On Being a Deacon's Wife

On Being a Deacon's Wife

by Martha Nelson

Broadman Press
Nashville, Tennessee

61,189

A COMMENDATION

When Martha Nelson speaks of "the potential of the marriage team, especially as it relates to the church," she indicates that she understands the plus dimension of the committed home. "Understand the office," she pleads; this is the basic prerequisite of becoming the teammate of her deacon husband. The theme of her book is seen when she writes, "Never underestimate the inspiration a mature Christian woman can be to her husband."

The warm human give-and-take of a home is suggested by her titles: "Be Yourself" and "Let Him Be." The book provides real promise to the deacon's wife caught up in the anticipation of her husband's commitment.

The wife's "what-do-I-do" question is answered well in the chapter entitled "Your Supporting Role." Here are many wonderful suggestions that can enrich the life of such a woman. The book is a delight to read, a helpful guide, and a warm promise worth the effort.

ROBERT E. NAYLOR

President
Southwestern Baptist Seminary
Fort Worth, Texas

PREFACE

It is impossible for a woman to give intelligent support to her husband without some knowledge of his vocation. As business and industry are well aware, the wife of an employee can be his most important ally as she becomes acquainted with his work.

Likewise, the wife of the deacon will be able to give significant support only as she understands the role her husband assumes with ordination. If she is to be supportive in his "other vocation," she needs to think in terms of how she may enhance and encourage his service as a deacon. This is a vast area, yielding opportunities for every kind of woman, whatever her skills and interests.

In a time when women are being urged to seek fulfilment apart from their husbands, it has been refreshing to explore the potential of the marriage team, especially as it relates to the church. I believe that the deacon and his wife who know a unity in their dedication to God can become a team with a tremendous potential for influence and service.

I know many wives who enjoy the role of helpmeet to their husbands. They like to feel they are complementing their husbands' personality and talents. Often they find their greatest personal satisfaction in doing things which are not a *duty* in the elective sense of the word. So I have sought to present some of the ways you as a deacon's wife might provide valuable support to your husband in his tasks of promoting harmony within the church and of ministering to persons in the name of Christ.

I first explored the subject with George Knight, editor of the magazine, *The Deacon*. Some of the material in this book originally appeared in two articles I wrote for that magazine, "A Special Word to Deacons' Wives" and "On Welcoming a New Pastor." Many ideas included here have come from other writers in *The Deacon*.

Through correspondence with deacons across the nation and in conversations with pastors, I have gleaned further suggestions. I have relied heavily upon *The Baptist Deacon* by Robert E. Naylor and Howard B. Foshee's *The Ministry of the Deacon*. Also, many deacons' wives and some pastors' wives have responded graciously to my queries.

As always, my husband Carl has worked along with me, providing invaluable suggestions as a pastor and theologian, and a husband's point of view as well. And my loyal friend Elsie Dozier—a deacon's wife who uses so generously in the Lord's service her previous experience as an executive secretary—insisted on typing the final draft of the manuscript. I am grateful to each person who has had a part in creating *On Being a Deacon's Wife*.

I'm excited about the opportunities awaiting you as you take your place beside your deacon husband. May the good Lord wonderfully bless both you and him as you discover the joys of being a *team* in his service.

MARTHA NELSON

CONTENTS

1.

Understanding His Role

*"The hope of the ministering church is
the informed, inspired, committed layman."*
Kenneth Chafin

Sitting through the closing moments of the ordination, Sarah Meyers was very proud of her husband Steve. She had known all along what a fine person she had married, and through the years she'd watched him grow in his Christian commitment. Now the people of their church were saying, "Here is a man we believe God can use as a special servant of the church." The ordination was a public expression of their respect and trust.

At the same time she felt a deep sense of humility. She was aware of her husband's weaknesses, and her own. She knew that neither of them could boast of having "arrived" as Christians. A sense of unworthiness and inadequacy crept over her.

Yet she felt an inexpressible joy and wonder in anticipation of the way this honor and responsibility might affect their future. She knew that rewards were in store if she and Steve were faithful.

Bowing her head, she brushed aside a tear. Within, a prayer groped for words—an offering of her beloved one to God, a thanksgiving for their togetherness in the Lord, a personal rededication, a plea for strength and wisdom. Her thoughts turned to the church and God's plan for his people, and she contemplated her own place in that plan.

Just then she heard, "We'd like the wives of these men to come

11

now and stand beside their husbands." Leaving the children beside Steve's proud parents, she moved from the pew to take her place at her husband's side.

There was no time now for further thought. People were pressing forward to greet them, to wish them well, to pledge their support and prayers.

Only a very cold and uncaring woman could sit through her husband's ordination without experiencing something of the pride, humility, joy, and prayerfulness Sarah felt that day. For ordination is a new kind of commitment for a man. It is a lifelong vow. It is the beginning of a highly responsible relationship to God and his people.

A woman from Kentucky, wife of a sincere Christian and outstanding deacon, said: "One of the greatest joys and blessings —and privileges—of our nearly fifty years of married life came to us the night my husband was elected deacon of Walnut Street Baptist Church. We always considered it a trust, not from the church but from God."

Intimating that she too had felt the touch of God's hand upon her life at that time, she continued: "It is true he was the one elected, but a deacon cannot give of his best if his wife is not in accord with his calling. Sad to say, I have known some who are not."

To experience that accord with his calling, a woman needs to understand the role her husband assumes with ordination. Hopefully, the church has carefully explained the qualifications and the tasks of its deacons, and husband and wife have made a joint decision in granting the church's wish to place his name in nomination. Otherwise, what is considered an honor at the outset may become a source of disillusionment to both deacon and wife, and to congregation as well.

Congregations, pastors, and deacons themselves have varying

concepts about the deacon's role in the life of a church. In your own experience you may have come across some of these varied concepts.

You may have grown up in a church where the deacons acted as a "board of directors," screening all recommendations and serving as "preacher prodders." Or you may have been in a church where the deacons were primarily business managers, seeing to the secular side of church affairs and leaving spiritual matters up to the pastor.

Your Uncle John may have been a deacon who understood his job to be "to serve the bread and wine and tell the preacher when to resign." Or you may have belonged to a church whose deacons were elected to pass the offering plate and pitch in a few extra dollars when the budget was tight.

You may know of churches where apparently the deacons' major responsibility is to march down the aisle to their reserved section at the front of the auditorium on Sunday morning, signifying their support of the man in the pulpit and their exemplary conduct to the people in the pew.

You may now belong to a church whose deacons are active in the pastoral ministries of visiting and counseling and serving people in a hundred caring ways. This concept is growing in popularity, and really, it is a return to the biblical pattern. Deacons and their pastors are excited about this new yet old emphasis—that the deacon is a servant of people on behalf of God in much the same way as the pastor.

Not only deacons, but other laymen are saying they are fed up with "playing church" and are anxious to get at the business of doing the kind of work the Lord commanded his disciples to do. In churches of all denominations there is a renewed emphasis upon the vital role of laymen in the growth of the church. Elton Trueblood, the noted Christian philosopher, says, "The rise of the layman is the great new Christian fact of our century." [1] And predictions are that the next ten years will bring churches to a full acceptance of the pastoral ministries role of the deacon.

It is logical that the intelligent, modern American male would want to be more than a church maintenance man! To assign duties relating to church finance and building and grounds, as vital as they are, to the deacon as his *primary* task leaves him wondering: Well, why all the talk of being doctrinally sound and full of the Spirit? Is this all I've been ordained for?

But make a deacon a yokefellow-in-ministry with his pastor, and he assumes a different attitude. Today's Christian man is challenged by this kind of opportunity. Proof of the fact is that thousands are gathering to train for service in pastoral ministries. They are studying how to witness, how to comfort, how to counsel. They are taking off by car and plane to share their testimony of God's power with Christians in distant places. They are taking the initiative in ministering to the people of their congregations, leading out in innovative ministries to disadvantaged and beaten-down people, giving aggressive leadership in making God's people a caring community of believers. And God is blessing their efforts.

"Being a deacon is not a title of honor," asserts Owen Cooper, a prominent Southern Baptist deacon. "It is a badge of servant-hood." [2]

In the New Testament the Greek word *diakonos* is translated "deacon" five times and twenty-five times "minister" or "servant." It literally means "through dust." Howard B. Foshee, in *The Ministry of the Deacon,* says the concept of raising dust suggests a servant hastening to serve or wait on his master. [3]

The deacon is not the pastor's servant! Like every other believer, he is the Lord's servant, and as a deacon, more specifically a servant of the Lord's church. Both pastor and deacon are specially set apart by God and his people for ministering. They are co-workers, part of a local church team.

The servant role is very clearly indicated in the Scriptures. The key story in Acts 6:1–5 begins like this:

"During this period, when the disciples were growing in number, there was disagreement between those of them who spoke Greek and those who spoke the language of the Jews. The former party complained that their widows were being overlooked in the daily distribution. So the Twelve called the whole body of disciples together and said, 'It would be a grave mistake for us to neglect the word of God in order to wait at table. Therefore, friends, look out seven men of good reputation from your number, men full of the Spirit and of wisdom, and we will appoint them to deal with these matters, while we devote ourselves to prayer and to the ministry of the Word' "(NEB).

And so the seven were elected, among them the mighty Stephen, a man of faith and power, and Phillip, a highly convincing Spirit-led witness. Though these men were not called deacons, it is generally agreed that the election of the "seven" was the beginning of the deacon as a church officer.

Note the two purposes of their election—to restore harmony and to help the apostles. Deacons were needed in that early church and certainly no less today!

We will always need men to work toward unifying the people of a church, for Satan is hard at the task of dividing them. "The one inescapable duty of the deacon in the New Testament was the protection of the church fellowship," says Dr. Naylor in *The Baptist Deacon*. "When things arise that are divisive it is time for a deacon who believes the Book to stand up and say, 'We cannot do it this way in this church. We must have harmony and peace if we are to honor Christ.' "

He says: "When a man becomes a deacon, he loses the privilege, if such exists, of participating in a church row. A member in the ranks may claim that often-abused privilege, 'speaking his mind.' When a man becomes a deacon—selected and called by the Holy

Spirit, chosen by a church, dedicated by personal choice, he forfeits the right to promote, in any fashion, a division in the life of the church." [4]

As a wise old minister said to me: "Deacons should be a part of the answer, not a part of the problem! The first deacons were chosen to solve problems, not create them."

A second purpose for the election of the seven was to designate certain well-qualified men as assistants to the apostles in ministering to evident needs.

One does not have to stand around a busy church office very long before it is clear that many of the calls coming in cannot be neatly categorized under any one person's, or organization's, responsibility. The wife of an alcoholic, an unemployed executive, one teen-ager hooked on drugs and another at a stalemate with his parents, a bereaved husband, a divorcee looking for a job, a transient family of ten looking for housing, a shabby old man needing a few dollars to tide him over . . . Who can help? Who will help?

The church needs compassionate, informed, inspired, and committed laymen willing to put their experience, wisdom, and connections in the community to work on such problems. By no means is the pastor always the man best prepared to meet the need of the hour, nor will time allow him personally to meet each need coming to his attention.

In all but the small church, it is impossible for the pastor to know all the people intimately, but deacons can take an interest, on behalf of the church, in certain families, providing the caring so needed in our highly impersonal world. In Chapter 7 we will discuss the systematic efforts some deacons are making in this regard.

Then always there will be families out of fellowship with the church. Deacons can frequently arbitrate successfully. If your pastor has caught a vision of how laymen can help, he may be calling upon your husband to give him a hand with many a sticky situation.

Deacons can take up where the pastor must leave off in ministering. For as new crises arise, the pastor cannot continue giving extensive support to individuals recuperating from crisis. For example, C. W. Brister, in *People Who Care*, tells of a devoted deacon whose wife died unexpectedly. This man acknowledged that the four-thousand-member church to which he belonged failed him during that grief experience. "I walked the streets of our city at night," he confessed, "so lonely I was tempted to seek fellowship with individuals in the bars and cheap hotels. No one knows what a wilderness experience that was!" [5] Fellow deacons and their wives could have eased that man's loneliness and despair. A continuing ministry was needed.

If the people of a church are knowledgeable of the Scriptures, they will expect the deacon to live up to the qualifications listed in 1 Timothy 3:8–13:

"Deacons, likewise, must be men of high principle, not indulging in double talk, given neither to excessive drinking nor to money-grubbing. They must be men who combine a clear conscience with a firm hold on the deep truths of our faith. No less than bishops, they must first undergo a scrutiny, and if there is no mark against them, they may serve. Their wives, equally, must be women of high principle, who will not talk scandal, sober and trustworthy in every way. A deacon must be faithful to his one wife, and good at managing his children and his own household. For deacons with a good record of service may claim a high standing and the right to speak openly on matters of the Christian faith" (NEB).

Congregations assume that its deacons will be active participants in the life of the church, loyal and stable, concerned with its total welfare and progress.

Deacons provide stability to churches. Pastors come and go,

as do elected officers of program organizations. But deacons can provide a continuity of leadership which prevents the church's lapsing into inactivity and despair in times of stress and uncertainty. Even in churches using the rotation plan, this continuity is maintained, for as some men complete their term of service, others with experience and seasoned wisdom remain to carry forward the plans and aspirations of the church.

Ordinarily, deacons have no authority other than to implement the decisions of a congregation. In times of emergency, however, they do have a kind of unwritten authority to assume leadership and to act in keeping with what they believe to be in the best interest of the whole church.

A big order? Indeed it is! But apparently your church believes your husband to be the kind of man who can handle it. And with you by his side, in full accord with his calling, he will be a tremendous asset to the church.

As the wife of a respected leader, you have a distinctive contribution to make also. In fact, here in the husband-wife team may lie your most challenging opportunity for Christian service.

There's power in *team*. The Lord promised it when he said, "If two of you shall agree on earth as touching anything that they shall ask, it shall be done for them."

There's companionship in *team*, for the word suggests mutual interests, a common goal.

Team carries the idea of sharing. You will have strengths and resources which will enhance those of your deacon-husband as he goes about his tasks of ministering and promoting harmony among God's people.

Team in the marriage partnership implies love. And love, someone has said, is two people looking in the same direction, two hearts tugging at the same load.

How splendid when that direction, that load, is God's work in this world!

2.
Be Yourself, Your Best Self . . .

"In human relationships, it is much more important to be the right person than to expect others to be so."
Ashley Montagu

Little Susie looked up at her mother during the laying on of hands in an ordination service and asked, "Mommy, why are they checking Daddy's head?"

Mother, with face appropriately straight, quieted her daughter with a whisper, "Why don't you ask the pastor after the service!"

So, one new deacon's wife had passed the test, "Must be grave" —and with flying colors!

Four qualifications for deacons' wives are listed in Paul's letter to Timothy. The King James Version of 1 Timothy 3:11 reads, "Even so must their wives be grave, not slanderers, sober, faithful in all things."

Modern translations and paraphrases give a break to the spirited women who insist, "But I'm just not the 'grave' type." Some read "honorable"; others "serious-minded," "sharing their husbands' serious outlook," "of high principle." The work of the Lord is serious business, not to be taken lightly. Church leaders should have a deep reverence for spiritual matters. This does not mean one must be long-faced, with no sense of humor. In church life, as in every other area of life, there are times when if you couldn't laugh, you'd surely cry!

The word also means "dignified in conduct." These days when so many women are casual to the point of carelessness, this interpretation seems highly appropriate. A woman of dignity has a poise and self-respect which inspires the respect of others. Homes and churches and communities need women of dignity.

The second qualification, "not slanderers," is inescapably clear. Malicious gossip is always a detriment to good, and both husband and wife are admonished to be careful about what they say. The deacon's wife must be discreet because even though deacons may pledge to keep a matter quiet, we know what Dr. Naylor says is true, "There are few deacons and no preachers who can avoid going home and talking to their wives about church troubles." The problem of communication is so vital we shall give it special attention in a later chapter.

"Sober," the third qualification, may seem completely superfluous for the Baptist woman brought up in a tradition of total abstinence. While one translation reads "not heavy drinkers," several others use the word "temperate." "Self-controlled" is even better, I think, for self-control covers a multitude of women's sins, from overindulgence in eating to plain old laziness.

The final qualification Paul mentions is "faithfulness in all things." A man in a position of spiritual leadership will be hampered by a giddy, fickle, frivolous girl of a wife. He needs a woman of constancy by his side. The deacon's wife should be completely trustworthy, a woman to be relied upon.

Dignified . . . discreet . . . self-controlled . . . altogether reliable. Whether she be blonde, brunette, or greying, size twelve or twenty, here is a woman to be respected and admired. Actually Paul advises against the ordination of any man whose wife might embarrass either him or the church. For a woman's behavior reflects upon her husband and, particularly if he is a church leader, upon the church. Paul had evidently seen troubles that result when a deacon's wife was an inconsistent Christian. He considered the matter sufficiently important to mention it in his second brief letter to Timothy.

The problem that has plagued ministers' wives through the years may nag at the sincere wife of a deacon. "How can I ever live up to all the expectations of all the members of the congregation?"

Wives who know say: "Don't try! It's impossible! Just be yourself."

A Texas pastor's wife, characterizing an ideal deacon's wife, wrote: "She's just like any other 'ideal' wife—an authentic human being!"

So be yourself, your *best* self.

Aim for spiritual maturity. Begin by settling the matter of your relationship with God, if there's any question about it. If you've been earthbound by doubt because your conversion experience was not of the dramatic Damascus-road variety, set yourself free. I've shared Kenneth Chafin's description of the different ways different people become Christians with a number of women anxious about the reality of their faith.

He says: "Some are reared so much in the context of the church that they cannot remember when they first believed. Others look upon their conversion as a growth process, while others experience a sudden change in their lives. Some had an early experience as a child and an affirming experience as a young person or an adult. The real test is not the type of experience but the *relationship* to which it leads. A person who believes that Jesus Christ is the Son of God and has, of his own free will, committed his life to Him, to live for Him in the context of His church, is a child of God." [1]

Recognize your need to grow. "Woman without spiritual wings is a dismal worm," says Adela Rogers St. Johns in her inimitable newsroom style.[2] Every Christian needs to grow, and until she does she'll remain wrapped in a seemingly lifeless cocoon. And who wants to remain "a dismal worm" when wings await her!

Prerequisite to growth is self-surrender. The growing Christian must put—and keep—self in its proper place. I know that womanly submission is not so popular these days. Yet Jesus said that is exactly where his disciples must begin. He indicated that any man or woman who wants to be his disciple must say "no" to self and, again and again putting aside personal desires and comfort, stay close to him, submissive to his will.

And, oh, does this take unselfishness! It takes unselfishness for a woman to permit her husband to serve his church in his spare time. It takes unselfishness to be faithful in attendance at worship when the call of the outdoors comes through so loud and clear week after week. It takes unselfishness to say no to the wide variety of self-satisfying weekday activities which result in Sunday morning exhaustion. It takes a great generosity toward God and others to tithe cheerfully. But until the wife of a dedicated Christian servant can say unreservedly, "Okay, Lord, here we are—use us," she is of all women most miserable.

When you've let go of self, then let yourself grow. Take advantage of the divine nourishment so readily available. Open that Bible and let God speak. Concentrate on the pattern you see in the life of Christ and copy it. Don't become quickly impatient nor too soon discouraged, for visible growth takes time.

Growth takes effort, too. God waits upon you to do your part. You know as well as I that we women can sing a hymn (even a solo), open our Bible, fix our eyes upon our pastor or teacher—go through all the motions of study and worship—without being the least bit nourished spiritually. Sitting there in body only, our minds far away in some department store or garden shop, we do not absorb the nourishment so vital to Christian growth. Wearing ourselves to a frazzle doing heaven-only-knows-what ("and I haven't a thing to show for it!"), we come to church so exhausted that not even God can get through to us with wisdom and strength for the week ahead.

Peter says in his second letter that we must work hard for spiritual growth, *"Giving all diligence,* add to your faith. . . ." Christian growth is so much more than the initial act of trust; it is faith supplemented by intelligence, self-restraint, perseverance, devotion to God, and lovingkindness to others.

Now that you're growing, relax! Watchman Nee tells us that God invites us to sit down and enjoy what he has done for us.[3] We don't feel strain and tension when we are with family and beloved friends. Our assurance of their love allows us to relax in their presence—there is no need for pretense, no need to fear.

God loves us, too, even more so. He made us, he knows us. And he has created each of us unique. We're "originals" at birth. With the new birth, he begins to add the finishing touches.

Health, physical stamina, emotional stability, mentality, talents, interests, skills, knowledge, understanding, experience, education, spiritual maturity—all that you have become "under the circumstances" combine to make you the one and only *you.* Family responsibilities and relationships contribute to your uniqueness. In no other woman will you find duplicated an exact mix of those factors which make you *you.* And the *you* you are today is not the *you* of yesterday nor tomorrow nor next year. So be yourself and relax in his presence and in the presence of others.

Consider yourself primarily responsible to God. Report to him regularly, neither measuring yourself against another human being nor concerning yourself too much about what others may say of you.

Put the major emphasis in your life upon *being.* Neither agility nor ability is the measure of a Christian. Granted, it's easier to measure a life by good deeds rather than attitudes. But the good deed minus the wholesome attitude remains questionable. Circumstances may limit your activities from time to time, but they need never limit your attitude.

A pastor's wife from South Dakota says, "I think the greatest contribution a deacon's wife can make is in lending spiritual maturity to the congregation." Of the most mature deacon-wife team in their church she said, "We lean upon them to help us bear problems that we would not dare breathe to other members."

The Spirit-fruit of maturity is essential in church relationships. We need love, for all God's people are not exactly lovable. We need joy, for disappointment is sure to come. We need peace when things occur which unsettle a congregation. We need patience, for the Lord does not always work in a hurry. We need gentleness, for hurting people must be handled so carefully.

Finally, if you haven't done so already, I'd suggest that you seek out your "gift." "Each of us has something to give that no one else can give," says Elizabeth O'Connor in *Eighth Day of Creation—Gifts and Creativity.*[4]

It is an important teaching of the Bible that each of us is endowed with unique gifts from God. "Each one must order his life according to the gift the Lord has granted him . . ." Paul writes in 1 Corinthians 7:17 (NEB).

What a pity to go through life without ever knowing of a single gift God has bestowed upon you! What a delightful experience to discover where you can excel! What pure joy to come to the place where, having developed your gift and put it to use, you can look upon its results!

In an article titled, "Discovering Your Gifts and Calling Forth the Gifts of Others," John Hendrix suggests ways of getting at one's gifts.

Write down all the strengths you think you have, he says. Include your interests, skills, and experience. Jot down your hang-ups, your inhibitions. Think of the things which have captured your interest and given you much personal satisfaction.

Then, talk to others about the possibilities for using these strengths. Find out what you can about various opportunities for expression to see if your unique gift may be "right" for them.

Label your gifts and begin to practice them. See how others react when you use them. Relate your gifts to the lists found in Romans 12:6–8; 1 Corinthians 12:4–10, 28–30; Ephesians 4:11; and 1 Peter 4:10–11.[5]

Then I'd suggest that you concentrate on your specialty. In our homes we cook, sew, clean, garden, do needlework, etcetera, etcetera, etcetera. Most of us have our favorite homemaking tasks (and all of us have our *chores*). We envy the homemaker who does something especially well: the one who turns out pies by the dozen and loves doing it; another whose home is made lovely with her needlepoint; yet another whose lawn is a veritable Eden. And some of us have to turn back to ourselves, with no specialty at all, and wonder "why?" Is it because of lack of sustained interest and effort? Or that we're just confirmed dabblers? Or because we've convinced ourselves we're mediocre, with no hope of excelling?

There's a smorgasbord of opportunity awaiting the woman who'd like to use her gifts in the Lord's work. But too many of us, I fear, dabble—here a little, there a little—never settling down long enough to become really expert at anything, while our Christian ministries suffer terribly from lack of expertise.

I believe the Christian woman needs to gain self-identity in the Lord's work. A husband and wife need to stand together but, as Gibran says, "not too near together: For the pillars of the temple stand apart, And the oak tree and the cypress grow not in each other's shadow." The satisfaction derived from personal acts of devotion can carry a woman through those times when her deacon-husband is deeply absorbed in the duties which are his and his alone.

What strength a spiritually mature woman can be to her husband and their church! A deacon from Missouri said: "I have a *good* wife. In fact, she is to be credited largely with making me the kind of man who might be asked to serve as a deacon. She continually inspires the best in me morally and spiritually."

One from Virginia wrote: "I consider myself fortunate in having a wife who is far more dedicated and service-minded than I. She does not consider service a chore but delights in it as an opportunity to do something for our Lord."

And a physician from Louisiana: "Most of all my wife has helped me by living an exemplary, consistent life every day of the week, reflecting positively upon me in every way."

Never underestimate the inspiration a maturing Christian woman can be to her husband!

Your deacon husband is going to need you. So be yourself, your best self!

3.
Let Him Be

"Marriage is not a reform school."
David Edens

"Deacons are human and none of them perfect," an Oklahoma deacon's wife said emphatically.

It's true, that illusory halo hovering over husband's head at his ordination soon fades in the everyday hustle of family living. And unless a wife has arrived at that happy state of accepting her mate for what he is, she may be tempted to chide, "Now that you're a deacon, dear. . . ."

Or, on the other hand, she may be tempted to tamper with his desire to serve on behalf of the church. A denominational leader who plans clinics for deacons says he recently received a call from a pastor asking him to conduct a session for wives, too. "Sometimes," the pastor said, "men make a commendable decision in their meeting, but when they get home, wives influence them otherwise, dampening their spiritual enthusiasm."

A deacon from Louisiana underscored such a possibility when he wrote, "My wife *allows* me to carry out any tasks I assume."

And confirming the fact that wives have been known to be obnoxious in their efforts at improvement, a St. Louis deacon laughingly expressed fear that this book would suggest ideals some wives would wield like a rolling pin over their husbands' heads!

As staunchly as most women support their church's belief in

religious liberty in the church-state arena, not all are willing to grant such freedom on the home front.

Sometimes wives *can* help husbands do better—and we'll get into that in later chapters—but it is also a fact that some women enter marriage thinking of it as a reform school, and failing at early reforms, they may pounce upon the ordination as a signal to renew their efforts. Assuming the role of "spiritual motivators," they allow their motivation to deteriorate into nagging and criticism.

The reforming drive (or to put it more nicely, the desire to *re-design*) is very strong; in fact, a marriage and family expert says it is "one of the most grievous dangers" in any marriage. We would be resorting to wishful thinking to assume that all Christian marriages have reached that blissful plateau where partners unconditionally accept one another *as is*.

Not that these are poor marriages necessarily, rendering husband and wife ineffective Christians. Sometimes one or the other may "lose himself" in church work to escape frustrations at home. Nor that they are completely unhappy. As Cowper wrote a long time ago,

> The kindest and the happiest pair
> Will find occasion to forbear;
> And something everyday they live,
> To pity and perhaps forgive.

But if one could look behind the smiling facade many Christian couples present to the world, one would no doubt find some unresolved conflicts.

Paul Plattner, in *Conflict and Understanding in Marriage*, points out that extensive investigations of married couples have revealed that in at least seven out of every ten marriages the partners differ markedly in a number of ways, both physical and psychological.[1] Of course, these differences are bound to express themselves in religious practice, too. In fact, one widely quoted student of masculine and feminine differences says women are even tempted to *sin* differently from men!

The wife who takes it upon herself to whip her newly elected deacon-husband into what she considers the proper deacon-image may, unwittingly, drive him farther away from, rather than closer to, what God has in mind for him to become.

And, in contrast, the wife who takes an opposite stance and hinders her husband's doing what he believes needs doing may drive him to resignation. She may cajole and plead and cry into her pillow until he literally throws up his hands in surrender, saying, "What's the use?"—leaving the congregation to wonder why he does not accept another term of service. Or he may become so calloused to her complaining that, though he goes on his way, the rift in the marriage team widens dangerously. It might be surprising to learn how many deacons become dropouts because of wives who refuse to let them *be*.

Hopefully you can look back upon the time when you began to feel really free to be yourself (even less than your best self) with your husband. And hopefully he now enjoys that same security—your loving acceptance of the man that he is. Hopefully you can say with Alice Patricia Hershey, "My husband may not have any outstanding talents that the world would acclaim. But he is unique in that he is God's gift to me." [2]

Certainly this is the beginning place for genuine *team*—as husband and wife, recognizing their differences, permit each other to *be* and *do* what they consider their privilege and responsibility under God.

It isn't always easy. "A most difficult requirement of a deacon's wife, one that requires a great degree of personal dedication, is that she be willing to consecrate and contribute her husband to his work as a deacon," says Robert Naylor in *The Baptist Deacon*. He wisely reminds us that just as a new bride must learn to share her husband with his vocational responsibility, so the new deacon's wife must learn a similar lesson in sharing. "This is no thirty-day responsibility which he has accepted, but a way of life and a willingness to serve which he has entered for life. There will be inescapable demands made upon him because he is a deacon."

If you have been a deacon's wife for any length of time, you know that, besides regular meetings, there will be special meetings. Some will call your husband away from his family; other occasions will call for your presence beside him. A Mississippi executive praised his wife for her cooperation in this respect: "She is especially careful not to schedule engagements which conflict with my responsibilities as deacon. And she usually goes with me when this is appropriate."

Things will come up which require a change in family plans or an interruption to a pleasant evening. Others may delay his arrival home for dinner. I wonder, if Stephen were married, how his wife felt about his evangelistic efforts.

Howard Foshee says: "Serving with the pastor in meeting the spiritual needs of persons is not an easy assignment. Long hours are often required. Late in the night a telephone may ring at a deacon's home. Time may be spent seeking to help an alcoholic master his problems. Acts of benevolence become a regular part of a deacon's day." [3]

It is fascinating to read of some of the projects deacons and laymen have undertaken in their after-hours. Men in a Kentucky church give up their leisurely Sunday morning family breakfast in order to be at a nearby lake by 7:30 A.M. to conduct an early service for campers.

Deacons and other laymen in a church in Virginia, seeing the need for a downtown mission for lonely, outcast men, pledged to give time and financial support for the project and spent many evenings repairing, painting, and rewiring the property they rented. Many are still involved in the ongoing ministry, providing music, program and speakers, food and building needs, and maintenance.

In another church it was the deacons who discovered the needs of prisoners in a local prison camp and led their church in repairing good used recreation equipment for them. Those who played on the church softball team accepted their challenge for a game. All of this has led to opportunities to work with parolees in finding jobs and a place to live.

In a large Texas church some fifteen deacons share information with job-seekers and make referrals to various community agencies. Others spend much time in helping the pastor work with alcohol and drug dependents.

And deacons help one another. One group abandoned plans for a weekend training retreat to help a fellow-deacon move his brick house! It had been constructed by mistake on another person's land! Some forty men of that church worked on the project every weekend for over a month.

Behind the scene in most of these cases are interested wives. Wives who know how to adapt. Wives who have enough personal interests that they don't feel completely abandoned when husband is away. Wives who know how to keep hot food hot and cold food cold, and how to explain father's absence so Junior will be proud instead of hurt. Wives who have reached that point in maturity when they can ungrudgingly share their husbands with his after-hours interest, as well as his vocation.

Adaptability! The apostle Paul doesn't mention it, but what a wonderful quality for a deacon's wife to possess! In fact, it becomes a necessity if your deacon-husband really works at the job.

A successful young pastor from Arizona makes adaptability a privilege, however, as he says, "The deacon's wife is in a sacrificial spot."

Sacrifice implies giving up, *forfeiting something one values highly for the sake of someone or something considered to have a greater value or claim.*

Family time, because of its scarcity, has taken on a much higher value in our days than in years past. Most families are scattered during the day, and even though work and school hours may not be so long, commuting adds to the length of the separation. Seldom does a man's occupation permit any of his family to work alongside him—actually many families really don't know what "daddy" does. Work takes many men out of the home for days at a time, shuttling them across country on company business. Besides, there are unprecedented claims upon the family's leisure, and families of teen-agers find these separating them all too frequently.

It is easy to give up an evening with husband now and then if he is home most other evenings. It is harder—and more of a sacrifice—if his evenings at home are few or irregular.

But a man's service as a deacon may, in fact, help him retain his sanity, particularly if his work is highly confining, a world of dollars and cents in which it is easy to lose sight of persons. If he spends his day at a calculator or in some stultifying routine, your deacon husband may feel that his leisure time is the best part of his day, and he may find in these hours of service a sense of fulfilment which would otherwise be sadly lacking in his life. And if he's enthusiastic, he'll not think of what he does for God purely as more work, for "to an enthusiastic man, his work is always part play, no matter how hard and demanding it is."

So, within reason—and most wives are good at knowing where and when to "put the foot down"—and depending upon family needs, which will vary as the years pass, the deacon's wife does well to abide by her husband's decisions about the time he chooses to spend serving the Lord.

It seems to be terribly normal and natural for a woman to covet her husband's time, and sometimes the temptation to object to his plans may be overwhelming. I've done battle with this selfish urge myself. But a few years ago, through a modern American parable, I saw the problem from another angle. I saw so clearly the "greater claim" for which I was forfeiting some of the time I wanted to spend with my husband.

On an early March trip from St. Louis to Oklahoma City, we drove straight into a blizzard that left trucks jack-knifed across bridges, scores of cars in drifts at the roadside, and more than a thousand people stranded far from their destination.

The snow had begun to shut out the landscape as we drove onto the Will Rogers Turnpike. Visibility was limited to just beyond the right-of-way when suddenly, straining forward tensely, trying to see ahead, I exclaimed, "Carl! What's that moving over there?"

As we got even with the shadow at the snow-driven roadside we were able to make out the outline of a pickup stopping just inside a fence corner. Two cowhands were at the tailgate, struggling to get a little calf up onto the truck bed.

"It's a parable, a twentieth-century parable!" I said, and almost as one we caught its heavenly meaning.

"Yes," my husband said, "what man of you having an hundred cattle, if he lose one of them, doesn't leave the ninety and nine in the corral and go after the one that's lost till he finds it?"

"That little calf's life depended on those cowhands," I commented on the obvious. And, as we drove on thinking of that parable, I caught its meaning for *me*. I thought of the wintry evenings when I had tried to coax my husband to break his schedule of visiting, to stay instead close to the warmth of our hearth. And, in spite of my pleadings, he had gone on out into the night, as I knew all the time he would, determined in his efforts to seek out someone lost in life's storms.

Some of us who are servant's wives have to learn to let them go ungrudgingly. We may need to learn what sacrifice really is through rereading of the sacrificial lives of wives of great men whose cause has been science or medicine, politics or space exploration, or evangelism. Many of us don't really know the meaning of personal sacrifice.

Increasing amounts of leisure promised by the futurists could solve some time-use problems for the Christian family. Added time off-the-job might diminish tensions in homes where church responsibility must now be squeezed into very busy business schedules.

But as more and more Americans invest in second homes, boats, and skiing and camping equipment, and have increasing leisure to use them, new tensions are developing. Does one "stay or go" when there are conflicting church responsibilities?

Georgia Harkness, a noted Methodist theologian, makes a strong case for *staying* in her book *The Church and Its Laity*. Describing contributions the layman makes to the service of corporate worship, she lists regularity of attendance first. She believes "the health or sickness of a church depends to a very large extent on the regularity and fidelity of its members in attendance at the Sunday service of worship. . . . An intermittent come-and-go congregation of people who attend church only when they feel like it, or only when they like the minister, is seldom a strong church devoted to the service of God and the enhancement of human good." [4]

Another problem which is becoming more prevalent with the new leisure is moonlighting. Not realizing that time spent in one way cannot be spent in another, a wife might unknowingly hinder a man's service as a deacon by encouraging his taking a second job in addition to his main work.

Or, the wife may be tempted to line up "plenty to keep husband busy" in his off time, demanding that he serve her rather than God, crowding him so much at home that he pushes aside other responsibilities. Do-it-yourself home improvements have been known to keep entire families away from worship for weeks at a time. Then, some popular magazines are urging wives to give that husband his equal share—a good 50 percent—of responsibility for children, dishes, and housecleaning. The woman on a deacon-wife team will probably have to take such advice with a grain of salt!

Sometimes Christian service costs in actual dollars and cents. It costs to hire services around the home that might well be done by the man of the house *if* he had the time and energy. Sometimes it costs in terms of niceties, things which might be obtained at the expense of religious duty.

Christian families should not expect to keep up with the Joneses who neither tithe nor spend time in worship or service, the Joneses with their beautifully manicured lawn and their enviable weekends of leisure. The Bible is plain in its teachings about the cost of discipleship. Something has to *give* if we are to follow our Lord closely.

Deacons are expected to be leaders not only in the giving of their time and talents but of their means, too. Paul's qualification, "not greedy of filthy lucre," presupposes a wife who also is not greedy. Christian discipleship, while not demanding austerity, does require a nonmaterialistic approach to life. Generosity toward God must be preceded by a sense of what is most worthwhile in life on the part of both the deacon and his wife.

Your husband's strong interest in his deacon-service can pay rich dividends for both of you in later life. For the early or the "young" retiree can be a problem if he has had only his work to absorb his thinking. In *When Your Husband Retires*, Mollie Hart says a man needs "an interest, activity—call it what you will— that is big enough to satisfactorily fill the hole left in his life when business is subtracted . . . one interest deep enough, broad enough, strong enough, to save him from becoming that trying and pitiful creature, the retired man who truly and literally does not know what to do with himself. When one thinks for even a moment of all the insatiable needs of our hospitals, churches, charities, civic groups, town governments, young people, old people, it seems incredible that anyone should ever be at a loss for something important and fascinating to do, something nicely suited to his capacities, desires and talents." [5] Certainly, the dedicated deacon has "something important and fascinating" to which he is committed.

Now, the demands upon a deacon will vary from church to church. Sometimes when a deacon is not "deak-ing" it may not be his fault at all.

"The only thing my church told me when they ordained me was where to stand to take up the offering on Sunday morning and where to sit at the monthly deacon's meeting," one deacon said.

And another quipped, "My church didn't even tell me that. I guess we were too small for that kind of thing."

A denominational leader admits, "The only time we have talked to our deacons is before their ordination. We seem to think that because we've laid our hands on a man, he is supposed to know what to do. . . . Many churches default on training and guidance of these men." [6]

But more and more churches and associations, seeing the tremendous potential for God within laymen, are equipping them for deacon-service. Following the example of other churches, our church planned a ten-week deacon development course, using *The Ministry of the Deacon* as a primary resource. Led by a deacon during the church training hour, it included wives, as well as potential deacons and their wives. It has resulted in a heightened sense of responsibility for ministry, outreach, and fellowship on the part of these people.

The leadership role your husband assumes will be uniquely his. David H. Smith, in an article titled "How Deacons Lead," reminds us that no man possesses all the skills necessary to lead under all conditions.

One person initiates action by action, by getting started at doing what needs to be done. Another initiates action by communication, informing people and organizing them for action. Another is skilful at negotiating in important business matters.

Still another acts as a peacemaker; he is gifted at the art of healing breaches among members. Yet another knows how to make the right motion at the right time. And another, like a deacon in one of our former churches, a labor union official, applies his skills at arbitration in stormy business sessions.

Sometimes, says Mr. Smith, a man may be adept at disagreeing, and here he speaks not of the disagreeable objector born in the "kickative" mood, but of the man who gently questions actions in order to help the church arrive at wise decisions.[7]

Whatever your husband's gift—whether it is administration, helping in the common tasks about the church, or simply caring—proudly let him be. With eyes of love you will see in him splendid qualities that others will miss. Commend him for that motion well-stated. Comment on his good judgment. If he's been resourceful (like the deacons in a tiny rural church who discovered at the last minute that the offering plates were missing and, having no hats, resorted to shiny hubcaps borrowed from the parking lot), praise him. Pat him on the back privately when he has succeeded in smoothing over some precarious situation. If he's an initiator, don't discourage him—the Lord's church needs that talent. Be sympathetic when things aren't going as he feels they should. Let him know you appreciate his helping ministries to troubled families.

Like the good wife in Proverbs 31:11–12, be the kind of wife of whom it can be said as in *The Living Bible, Paraphrased*—"Her husband can trust her, and she will richly satisfy his needs. She will not hinder him, but help him all her life."

4.

Your Home in God's Service

"The profession of homekeeper, perhaps the noblest in the world, and the one that should be termed sacred if any is, lends itself to the establishment of centers of Christian influence."

Elton Trueblood

A good home can double a deacon's worth to the Lord and his church! Ask any good deacon how his wife has helped and he'll mention his home nearly every time.

"No one can serve adequately unless he has a happy home," one said.

"I think my wife has helped me most of all by making our home a pleasant place," another remarked.

And a third: "My wife adds so much to my everyday life. Perhaps that's where it counts most, for that's where my decisions and actions as deacon stem from, and where they're backed up."

A familiar quotation sums up the superlatives in Christian homemaking—

> The crown of the home is godliness;
> The beauty of the home is order;
> The glory of the home is hospitality;
> The blessing of the home is contentment.

Godliness, order, hospitality, and contentment—what a standard of living! A woman needs her Bible, her cookbook, plenty of elbow grease, determination, and all the tricks of the trade— plus love—to create such a place.

But it's not out of reach!

I've seen homes that measured up to that high standard in all sorts of places—on out-of-the-way plantations in Mississippi, in depressed areas of rural Oklahoma, in blue-collar suburbs of St. Louis and affluent suburbs in Denver, and on both sides of the track in small towns across the state of Texas. Regardless of economic or cultural levels, any Christian home—whose occupants really want to—can attain this splendid level of living.

According to this standard, the crowning quality of the Christian home is godliness. Yet I can't remember when I last heard a modern home described as "godly." Warm, lovely, attractive, charming—yes. But *godly*?

Too bad we've left so rich a word behind. Godly, according to the *American Heritage Dictionary*, means "having a great reverence for God." It's a word worth being reinstated in the Christian vocabulary. For the finest homes among God's people are built upon that "transforming triangle"—a husband, his wife, and their God.

Two young adults attending a lay evangelism clinic revealed the fact that young marrieds often shy away from the openness about spiritual matters which characterizes the godly home. They are a dedicated couple, active in church affairs, their home a base for a weekday morning Bible study. But at the conclusion of the training the wife said, "This week for the first time, my husband and I have begun to express to each other our deepest religious feelings and yearnings."

Because they have now learned to talk together about God and the Christian way, their young son will grow up knowing God not just as someone to be worshiped at church but as a very real person whom his parents know intimately, who is very much a part of his home.

In our casual American way of life even the table blessing has been laid aside by many Christian homes. Yet here is one of the simplest, most logical ways for a family to begin audibly expressing their reverence for God. In our home the mealtime blessing often extends into prayer for our church, for persons in trouble, for loved ones far away, for one another, and always for divine direction for our day.

Thus breakfast, lunch, and dinner table become an altar, a place where one or the other parent easily and naturally says, "Let's be thankful." And God is acknowledged and reverenced.

A deacon's wife suggests that "if there aren't family devotions in the home, the wife should lead out in establishing the practice." *Someone* must, and it may be easier for the woman to initiate the practice. This is *team*, you know, when one partner assumes a responsibility that moves both nearer their agreed-upon goal.

Godliness shows up in husband-wife, parent-child relationships; in attitudes and actions toward friends, enemies, in-laws, the folks next door, and the people in one's church. It comes through in the most everyday dilemmas about what is ethical and moral. It expresses itself through the kind of magazines and books lying about the house, and the kind of television shows the parents tolerate. It is evident as parents help children evaluate what they see and hear in the deluge of mass communication. It is seen in family recreation, in the kind of tourists the family become on vacation. It shows up in the spirit in which church work is accomplished and in the quality of that work.

Simply put, godliness is the practice of love, a way of behaving, a pattern for thought and conduct, a way of treating people.

It takes a great deal of skill and initiative for a family to live its religion today when the majority of the families in one's community go about as if there were no God. Never have children and youths of Christian families been so exposed to ungodly influences. Little wonder they sometimes rebel at their parents' ideals.

And deacons' kids are human, too. (You've probably heard why some are so bad—they play with preachers' kids!) Many of them grow up in church, indeed think of it as a second home! One little fellow, on being told to "hurry and get ready, it's almost church time," was heard to mutter as he moved to obey, "Chu'ch, chu'ch, chu'ch, that's all we ever do, go to chu'ch!" And others have surely felt like the pastor's four-year-old who prayed, after a week of evenings at church, "Dear God, I'm pooped!"

Most church-going mothers have shuddered at the thought of the naughtiness of their little sons in Sunday School or children's choir. But really, can we blame them if they feel so much at ease there? We have to remember that those dignified deacon husbands sitting so sedately in the church service were once wrigglesome, prankish little boys, and (shall we admit it?) we were once restless, whispering teen-agers going through that "do we have to be seen as a family?" stage. God has been gracious and patient with us, and while we certainly must keep on trying to make model children of our own, we can't afford to despair. To threaten them with "Remember, your daddy is a deacon!" may turn them forever from a leadership role in the church of their future.

Many deeply committed Christian parents have been embarrassed by the rebellion, waywardness, and indiscretions of their young. They have felt like hiding from friends at church, and some have dropped out, moving their membership or becoming inactive. But the parents in a home crowned with godliness remember how our Lord used a parent's love in his story of the prodigal to show us what love is really all about, and they stand firm through such crises.

The home marked by its reverence for God will naturally make the following of our Lord Jesus Christ its prime privilege and responsibility. And there is the beginning place, I believe, for *beautifying the home with order.*

For attractive and neat-as-a-pin a house may be, it can still be a far cry from possessing the kind of order most vital to the

Christian home. To read the house and garden magazines, one might get the idea that the artful arrangement of furniture and the creative use of accents mark the epitome of success in home-making. But to the contrary, as an ancient philosopher said, "The occupants should be an ornament to the house, and not the house to its occupants."

In his Sermon on the Mount, Jesus talked about the kind of order he was most concerned with: "Seek ye first the kingdom of God and his righteousness." He pointed out the anxiety and uneasiness we run into when we place too much value on appear-ances, possessions, and physical satisfaction. He tried repeatedly to help people gain a sensible, workable perspective on life.

Each of us individually must move into a position where we can get our Lord's perspective. The married pair, too, need to have understandings about what they believe to be the good life. Most newlyweds plan together the dream house they hope some-day to own. Fewer talk about what life means to them and what values they are living for, or dream of the kind of life they want to build together. Yet as Evelyn Mills Duvall says, "Nothing can bring greater satisfaction than finding that life all adds up, and that together the two know who they are and where they are headed in the business of living." [1]

The deacon and his wife who have never said much about their goals may find the time of ordination ideal for discussing them together. Then, decisions can be made in light of these goals, and an order can develop as the days grow into weeks and weeks into years. If there is to be *team*, there must be mutually agreeable goals. A couple can sacrifice serenely—and the Christian way calls for sacrifice—when they know where they are going in the process. This is the highest kind of order a home can possess.

But as important as the establishment of overarching life goals is to the people in a home, a woman must concern herself also with the practical day-by-day order that makes a home a happy place. This involves personal choices on her part—decisions about how much she can do outside the home at a given time, about what she wants, and about how the family's money should be spent. It will involve her guidance in the children's choices— the extent to which they can participate in organized activities like scouting, swimming, skating, horseback riding, and so on, without disrupting the family's participations in the life of the church. This is a real enigma when the leaders of these activities ignore church relationships of the youths in their charge. It will involve parental agreement over guidelines and limitations for the children.

And then, especially for the woman of the house, order means tidiness and careful scheduling. You've seen what disorder and confusion can do to a family—father leaving for work with a hastily bolted bowl of cold cereal instead of his usual hot break- fast; Junior knocking down the postman on his way out, only to return momentarily to announce, "Ma-a-a, I missed the bus"; you collapsing finally in sheer exhaustion.

You've seen the whole family driving grumpily to Sunday School because of a single, insignificant incident which threatens the spirit of an entire family.

These little insignificant somethings can so easily spoil an oth- erwise beautiful Sunday—or Monday—morning.

Recently, greeting a little preschooler on her way to Sunday School, I noticed her obvious unhappiness. "I'm mad at Mommy!" she asserted. And, as I wondered if I dared ask why, she went on, "I don't like this dress!"

It was really a pretty dress—soft pink, with a touch of applique and a fringe of dainty lace about the neckline.

"Why, it's lovely," I tried being helpful.

At that she wrinkled her face to make way for tears, and stamp- ing a little black patent shoe in frustration, she said, "But I keep telling Mother it doesn't have enough lace on it!"

Even superior management by the best of mothers can't alleviate an occasionally hectic morning. After all, deacons' wives are also human, and youngsters are highly unpredictable. If it's not one stage they're going through, it's another!

But, while Father provides the money to maintain the family, Mother is primarily responsible for the mood of a home. She must be a good organizer and supervisor, for *she* is top management at home, notwithstanding the fact that the husband "ruleth his house well" from his superior post as head of the house.

In my book, *A Woman's Search for Serenity,* I insist that life doesn't have to be so hectic! For I believe a woman can, by sheer will power, bring order out of the chaos of a busy home. By arriving at a sense of order within her own self, through planning, and even as she decorates the home, she can create an atmosphere of order and serenity. Whatever it takes, serenity in the home is worth her effort, for a usually-smoothly-running household is a backdrop for happiness.

It takes a woman with determination, imagination, and dedication to create an orderly home. Lines from the hymn, "Dear Lord and Father of Mankind," might well become the prayer of the woman who wants to make her home beautiful with order—

> Take from our souls the strain and stress
> And let our ordered lives confess,
> The beauty of Thy peace.

Most likely, the home crowned with godliness and beautified by order will be a hospitable home. Religious women have a long tradition of hospitality. There was Sarah who helped Abraham entertain angels unawares . . . the little woman who provided a room with a bed, table, stool and candlestick for the prophet Elisha . . . Mary and Martha whose home was always open to our Lord. And the man who loaned the upper room for the Last Supper probably had a wife who readied it.

Edith Deen, in *The Bible's Legacy for Womanhood*, says woman's home has been "a cradle for the church." [2] There was the church in the house of Aquila and Priscilla and in untold numbers of other Christian families. In nearly every case in the Bible where a man is named as having been hospitable to the church and its leaders, we may assume a woman in the background making ready. And there was Lydia of Thyatira, the seller of purple who urged Paul and his companions to abide in her house.

A deacon in one of the early churches might have said: "Get a big meal ready fast, honey. Paul and Barnabas are in town." Today's deacon is more likely to suggest, "How about our entertaining some of the newcomers to our church . . . or some of the families in my group?"

Through the years deacons and their wives have taken seriously the admonition in Romans 12:13 to be "given to hospitality." Yesterday's deacons' kids remember well the Sunday dinners and revival-time meals when the preachers came to their house. The homes of our grandparents housed itinerant preachers, denominational workers, and missionaries on furlough. Some deep and lasting impressions were made upon the children in those homes.

In rural churches served by college and seminary students, this kind of hospitality continues to be the tradition. But in many places the greater need is for a warm welcome extending from the homes of established church folks to uprooted families.

Today many homes which open their doors to fellowship Bible studies are really harboring little churches. A Texas church operates without a church building, not just as a temporary measure, but with "house churches," believing that we need to return to fellowship meetings in the home. Here and there churches with fine buildings are experimenting with the idea that laymen's homes may be the best place for lost and inactive people to gather with dedicated Christians to talk about spiritual matters.

Certainly one of the greatest needs in our churches today is fellowship, and here is where the feminine partner of the deacon team can shine. As one man said, "There's nothing quite like sticking one's feet under a fellow Christian's table for breaking down barriers to friendship." Churches may have picnics, receptions, and Wednesday evening suppers by the dozen—and these are much needed for our scattered congregations—but none of these quite equal a visit in the home over a cup of coffee for building a sense of fellowship between Christians.

This is not just "Christian," it's friendly! It's a way of saying "I like you" and "let's get better acquainted" or "I'd like you to meet some friends."

I spent a delightful hour recently with *Betty Crocker's Hostess Cookbook* with its many ideas for entertaining. In a letter to hesitant hostesses, the book urges, "Pick a party and start planning it now. . . . Don't let inexperience, shyness or a tiny kitchen stop you." [3]

And "don't just invite the preacher," says Elizabeth Swadley in *Dinner on the Grounds Cookbook*. "Invite each other. The new people you need to get better acquainted with, or the family you've always planned to have but haven't yet, or your Sunday School class, or some college students away from home, or some lonely soldiers you saw in morning worship." She adds, "I'm not convinced that there is any greater need today than the need for fellowship and love among Christians. We are going to have to make time and effort to rediscover each other, to accept one another, to love one another." [4]

There's no dearth of ideas for meals and refreshments. And with all the quick-and-easy's one can pick up at the supermarket, there's no excuse for even the busiest woman not entertaining now and then. If the welcome is warm and friendly, people could care less about whether what they are served was made from scratch.

Sometimes women don't want to make the sacrifice involved in hospitality. Our youngest daughter, a few months after she was married, pinpointed the fact of sacrifice after having her first weekend guests. "I've got a lot to learn about entertaining," she announced. "But I've learned one thing—it's work!"

Yes, my dear, it's work (I tried to tell you when you were younger). It's cleaning-work, and kitchen-work, and shopping-work, and then it's cleaning-up-afterward work. It's costly in time and energy and often in dollars-and-cents. But it's so rewarding when it's done in Christian love.

Actually some of the humblest homes are the most hospitable. It's true, "where there's room in the heart there's room in the home." I have been deeply impressed with the generosity of many deacons and their wives in opening their homes to others. One couple in St. Louis took an alcoholic into their home for weeks to help him overcome his desire to drink. The man they helped now has completed his seminary training and plans to devote his ministry to work with alcoholics.

Another family sheltered a young woman pregnant out of wedlock. And another forfeited their privacy to house an elderly man while he searched for permanent living quarters.

Many have extended hospitality to youths away from home. In the informal times of dining together and sharing a fireside, these young people, many from broken or badly damaged homes, have caught a glimpse of a stable marriage and a value system that is absolutely workable.

Yet there are many homes whose doors never swing open to others. Some women are fearful lest their cooking skills and home furnishings be compared and found wanting. As a student wife in a missions organization which included women from the finest homes in our town, I battled this kind of reluctance. But I swallowed my pride, cleaned like mad, and invited them to our basement apartment for a meeting.

Several years later a bit of Scripture taught me that perfection in home furnishings and table service should never keep one from being warmly hospitable. At the time we were sheltering a young woman who needed a place to stay while she got started on a job in Fort Worth. We were in an apartment and could only offer her a makeshift sleeping arrangement.

The words of our Lord spoke to my need as he said something like this to the apostles he was sending out, "If anyone gives even a cup of cold water to one of you, I tell you this, he will assuredly not go unrewarded."

For the first time it occurred to me that our Lord did not specify what kind of cup. It did not have to be fancy, nor even perfect. It might even be chipped!

So much I have had to offer in the way of hospitality through the years has been imperfect—the roast a bit overdone, the pie a little runny, the coffee sometimes too strong, or the tea too weak. The furnishings of our home are "American Providential," and sometimes our guests have had to share the family bathroom. Come to think of it, so much of everything I have to offer in the name of our Lord is imperfect.

But he said, "Give in my name—even a cup of cold water—and you'll be rewarded." He did not insist upon Haviland or Wedgwood or Lenox—just a cup. Even a chipped cup!

Of course if you have nice things, use them if you're in the mood. It's a way of honoring, of making your guests feel important. But if you haven't, use what you have with a flair and with love. Remember the little woman with only two mites whose giving so pleased our Lord.

It's a wonderful thing for a deacon's wife to enjoy being hospitable. For hospitality is the glory of the home!

Now, while a home might possibly be happy without order or hospitality, it can never be truly happy without contentment. The woman who can honestly say with the apostle Paul, "I have learned in whatsoever state I am, therewith to be content" will be a real boon and blessing to her deacon-husband.

The New Testament plainly teaches the value of contentment, "Godliness *with contentment* is great gain." Contentment, according to this statement, is a "plus" worthy of our best efforts.

Because so much feminine discontent stems from a desire for the material, for the things that money will buy, let's read from *The Living Bible, Paraphrased* what Paul writes to Timothy in 1 Timothy 6:6–10

> Do you want to be truly rich? You already are if you are happy and good. After all, we didn't bring any money with us when we came into the world, and we can't carry away a single penny when we die. So we should be well satisfied without money if we have enough food and clothing. . . . For the love of money is the first step toward all kinds of sin. Some people have even turned away from God because of their love for it, and as a result have pierced themselves with many sorrows.

The Christian woman at peace with herself is well equipped to create a spirit of contentment in a home. She has a healthy regard for herself as a child of God, for her importance and her worth as an individual. She has a sound, biblically based philosophy about material possessions. She doesn't spend a lot of time sitting around with negative people; she has a positive mental attitude and a sense of humor that stands her in good stead when "everything nailed down is comin' loose." She is in control of her life—determined to make the best of it. While she experiences mood downswings now and then, she is usually cheerful and optimistic. She has learned to graciously accept and to diligently work around those conditions which seem to be unchangeable.

Knowing she needs a sense of personal fulfilment, she uses her time creatively and does not rely solely upon her husband to bring the outside world in to her. She cultivates an attitude of gratitude and has learned to enjoy the little pleasures of life

which God has made available to all who will use their five
senses. Even though she may be poor by her community's stand-
ards, she's the kind of woman who feels that she has "everything
but money."

More than one deacon who wrote me regarding the content
of this book suggested I mention a man's need for sexual gratifica-
tion.

Out of his experience with disintegrating marriages a Texas
attorney said deacons' wives should be reminded of the importance of sexual fulfilment and a wholesome attitude toward sex.

One described a distressing situation where both husband and
wife were deeply involved in the life of their church (as they
should be, he indicated). "As the years progressed, however, the
wife became so involved that she had no time to fix meals for the
family and was too tired to participate in any sexual fulfilment
of marriage. The result was tragic for the marriage, the children,
and the church." He concludes that a deacon's wife should be
active in her church, but never to the point of neglecting her
husband and family.

And confirming the fact that breakdowns do occur within
dedicated church-related families, our local attorney said that he
has counseled more than one couple who had become overin-
volved in church activity to the hurt of their personal relationship. But a minister observes that the church should not be
blamed. No doubt there have been unresolved problems in these
marriages to begin with, and the church becomes first a place of
refuge, and finally the scapegoat.

Unquestionably, if there is to be contentment in the home, the
persons there need to feel loved—indeed, deeply cared for. They
need to feel secure, assured of a deep commitment to one another
even in the midst of disagreement. They need to be recognized.
As a family counselor said, "Sometimes when people in a home
misbehave, they are in reality saying: 'Attention! attention! I

need attention!' " (Someone has said when people act their worst is when they need to be loved the most.)

Family members also need to feel respected. They need to feel successful. And they need a place where they can find comfort, relaxation, and leisure. These are needs the emotionally mature woman can fulfil. She creates contentment as she communicates love, security, recognition, and respect to her husband and children.

Your husband may carry the key to your safety deposit box but you, his wife, carry the key to contentment in the home. If it's been misplaced, find it quickly. And use it daily so your home may enjoy the blessing of contentment.

What a wonderful fellowship we would know in our churches if every home were crowned with godliness, beautified by order, glorified by hospitality, and blessed with contentment! With divided loyalties it's an impossible dream. But when a deacon and his wife are really teamed up to the glory of God, there's no reason in the world why their home can't attain this high standard and be a shining example to the people of their church and community.

5.

Your Part in Pastor-People Relations

*"If only congregations would realize
that the perfect minister does not
exist, a good many heartaches might
be spared."*

Before her husband was ordained as a deacon, Sarah Meyers had never given much thought to the personal problems of ministers and their families. But at a statewide retreat her eyes were opened. Long after everyone else had turned in, she sat with Linda Young and Elsie Miller watching the dying embers in the great stone hearth of Greenwood Lodge. It's times like these, you know, when women who scarcely know each other loosen up and begin to talk of their hidden world.

Elsie was the wife of an educational director, the mother of four youngsters. "The six of us spend all week long going in different directions," she said. "There's scarcely a waking hour when one or the other isn't supposed to be at church! In fact, we go for weeks on end without finding a day when we can all get away to the lake together."

Linda, the young pastor's wife, nodded, "There are days at our house when our children never see their daddy. They probably think he lives at church! No one ever told me the demands made upon pastors—nor the demands they make upon themselves.

"Sometimes Bob is so burdened with problems he doesn't even hear what I say. It can be embarrassing, believe me, when a church member guesses *we* aren't communicating!"

With a break in her voice, she continued, "We're working

through a lot of our personal problems, of course, but I have to admit sometimes I feel resentments toward the church, the very people we know God has called us to serve.

"This summer while our Mark and Laura were at Mother's, I suddenly realized I had begun to wrap my life around the children—to the exclusion of Bob. He and I had a long talk about *us* and the kind of home we felt God would want us to have, and we're trying hard to create a more wholesome, normal home life. But it isn't easy."

As Linda and Elsie talked, Sarah sensed with unusual insight the constant daily pressures affecting a minister and his home. She visualized the pastor's diversity of tasks, the "tyranny of the should" he must grapple with daily, his vague hours, his being on call around the clock.

Remembering the emotional drain she and Steve had felt when they'd been confidantes of a deeply troubled couple, she imagined the emotionally exhausting load of confidences a pastor must carry. What a jolt it must be to go straight from a father rejoicing over a newborn to a mother grieving for a runaway daughter, from a morning funeral to an evening wedding.

She reasoned, "Other professional men have their career-related problems, too . . . but a minister can't schedule appointments weeks away when a couple's in trouble. He can't engage an answering service to screen his calls like a physician nor have the more urgent ones referred to a colleague when he is otherwise occupied. Nor can he close up shop like Steve and enjoy a complete change of scene over the weekend."

Elsie was saying: "There's just so much a pastor can't explain about how he spends his time. One person's problem can tear up an entire week's schedule, and that person may not even be one of his flock. And when he's spent hours counselling with a church family, he can't advertise the fact. In fact, he must work to keep it secret."

Sarah thought of the wives of these men. She recalled a *Good Housekeeping* article titled, "What Are You Doing to Your Minister's Wife?" The writer, a woman familiar with the distorting pressures of life in a parsonage, declares that some congregations are actually driving men out of the pulpit with their unreasonable expectations.[1]

Taken separately, each church member's expectation seems reasonable enough. Put them all together, however, and you have an impossible ideal.

Sarah had observed that most of the pastors' wives she'd known had avoided close personal friendships within their congregations, lest they create jealousies. Imagine not feeling free to develop close friendships at will within one's church!

Though their church provided adequate, comfortable housing —in fact a lovely home—for their pastor, Sarah had seen the monstrosities of dwellings some churches owned. Linda said theirs was a cold barn of a house and so in need of repair.

Sarah knew, too, of congregations that skimped in paying their pastors. Recently she had heard someone remark that "it really costs them less to live, what with no taxes or medical bills . . ." How could anyone be so ignorant! Of course ministers have these expenses; the "ministerial discount" is fast becoming a thing of the past.

She tried to imagine living in the public eye on a less-than-adequate budget. Yet today she had heard a hint of a criticism of a minister's wife who was employed. Some people are reluctant to grant that privilege to those wives who need or want to work, particularly if they are not trained for a prestige position.

She suspected that some pastors' wives go to work to get away from their telephone. It is a matter of survival. Ministers' wives, she thought, must experience a terrific emotional drain as they are drawn either directly or indirectly into the life crises of so many persons.

In these moments of insight, Sarah felt sympathy for the sensitive pastor's wife suffering a thousand hurts from the hostilities that crop up in churches sooner or later. . . .

Unwittingly, during that late evening fireside session, Sarah Meyers had taken the first step toward good pastor-people relations. She had begun to empathize with, to understand, the people in the parsonage. From then on she did everthing she could to influence others in her church toward a more loving, Christlike relationship with their pastor and his family. For understanding is the first law to be observed in the pastor-people relationship.

The second, acceptance, comes more readily when the first is observed. And key people in the local church, such as deacons and their wives, are in position to give leadership in genuine acceptance of the men the church may call.

The law of acceptance does not demand that one stop loving a former pastor. When he has participated with you in the joyous ceremonies of life, been intimately concerned with your problems, and watched with you in sorrow, it may take two or three years for the transfer of love and respect to another spiritual leader to take place completely.

The sense of dependency upon a pastor, however, should terminate with his leave-taking and the new pastor welcomed with every assurance that he can count upon your personal loyalty, good will, and prayers. Then he can proceed unhindered, to take up where his predecessor has left off and begin to make his own place in the hearts of the people.

The law of acceptance forbids the incessant praising of previous ministers and their wives. All it takes to depress a new man and his wife is the reminder: "What a giant in the pulpit, tremendous organizer, tireless visitor, remarkable man our *last* pastor was—and his *wife*, an angel if ever there was one. . . ." Nobody enjoys succeeding a saint! Nor will they appreciate frequent allusions to their predecessor's weaknesses with the subtle implication, "We're counting on you to be different."

You can rest assured the conscientious minister and his wife are already deeply aware of their own inadequacies and limitations. Most ministers expect a great deal of themselves, and experts say many ministers' wives assume their role haunted by the stereotypes suggested in unrealistic fiction and idealistic books written by and for their own kind. Further suggestions will only add to their tensions.

The people of a church may need to be reminded that ministers are not super-humans. And that no one of them will excel in every facet of his position. One may be expert at counseling, another in crisis ministries, another as an administrator, another as an evangelist, another as a teacher. The very differences in spiritual leaders can help develop a strong church.

"If the congregation can accept these differences, much like one accepts design, pattern and color shading in the beauty and richness of fabrics, then all concerned can beautify their lives as persons and as a congregation," notes a prominent pastor in a *Pastoral Psychology* article.[2]

The mature congregation accepts the glories and the weaknesses of each of its ministers and goes on, rather than fighting the personality differences each brings to his position.

As you look for your minister's strong points and assume that God is using him to accomplish his purposes for your church, you can put a stop to a lot of nitpicking with a good word in the pastor's behalf.

The minister's wife, too, needs your acceptance—of her cultural and educational background, her experience, her pace and her concept of her role. The highest compliment you may pay her is to indicate you have a genuine interest in and respect for her as a woman, a person with thoughts, feelings, insecurities, and aspirations much like those of any other woman.

Ministers' wives find they must be themselves if they are to adjust to parsonage living. A few fulfil a kind of "assistant-pastor" role, but according to Wallace Denton and William Douglas, both of whom have studied the problems of ministers' wives, this type seems to be passing from the scene.[3] Many ministers strongly resent congregations looking for a one-cent sale—you know, "Pay for one, get a second for a penny." They do not want their wives acting as their unpaid assistants.

Most ministers' wives feel that no more should be expected of them than of any other Christian woman, though of course they expect to be more involved than the average member. They feel their greatest contribution is through background support of their husbands and their participation through their husbands. Most can be counted on, however, to serve as Sunday School teachers, to work with the women of the church, and to use the talents they have.

Here and there you will find wives who detach themselves from the work, feeling no more compulsion to be involved than if their husbands were in another vocation. A few resist involvement, withdrawing out of rebellion against the demands made upon their time and energy by their husbands and/or the congregation. Some seem to need privacy, anonymity, or a second life, more than others.

Dorothy Harrison Pentecost, in her book, *The Pastor's Wife and the Church,* suggests that if you notice defensiveness or other unhealthy attitudes developing in your pastor's wife, "instead of criticizing her, try to find out what is causing the trouble and do your best to straighten it out. Show her kindness and appreciation, and release her from so many demands and expectations. You have already lost a pastor's wife if she feels this way, and you can be well on your way to losing a beloved pastor if it continues."[4]

However your minister and his wife fulfil their roles, they

need your acceptance. Your example will inspire others to live **by** this Christlike law.

The third law I'd suggest for good pastor-people relations is the law of kindness. For acceptance *per se* can be cold, while acceptance with kindness looks behind actions for reasons and tries to ease the problem. Kindness makes one gentle with those who are troubled and ill-adjusted because of inexperience, youthful immaturity, or lack of preparation for their role. Many a fine pastor and his wife look back fondly upon a mature, kindly deacon-wife couple who acted as spiritual advisors to them in their youth.

Kindness gives others the benefit of the doubt. I believe it is expressed most beautifully in a generosity of attitude toward other Christians. It is not judgmental.

Kindness shows itself in little acts of thoughtfulness. It is much appreciated when the minister and his family are newcomers to a community. Deacons' wives can do much to make the early days following a move a little easier. It may be in the thoughtful planning and provision of a few meals at the outset, in seeing that the house is clean and readied for occupancy, in caring for the children during the hectic rush of getting settled, in providing a place to eat and sleep until furniture arrives or, if he is on a housing allowance, until a house is located.

The deacons' wives may see that appropriate plans are made for introducing the family to the church. The traditional all-church reception might be supplemented by smaller, more intimate get-togethers. Newcomers to a church staff are bewildered at first by the dozens of names and faces to be sorted, paired, and coordinated so rapidly.

Soon after our arrival at our present church, the wives of the deacons planned a supper, one of those you-bring-the-salad-I'll-bring-the-pie-and-we'll-all-pitch-in-on-the-ham affairs. Instead of having the supper at the church, a deacon and his wife offered their home and we went into a warmly hospitable setting, small tables scattered about, candles and seasonal flowers creating a festive air of welcome. The buffet was especially palatable in the delightful atmosphere of that home.

Afterward as we sat down to chat in the living room, the host suggested that everyone share something about himself to the entire group. Talk ranged from "where I'm from" and "where my wife and I met" to careers and hobbies and of course "our unusual grandchildren." There was jolly laughter and a bit of good-natured ribbing, with an easy friendliness characterizing the entire evening. In our suburban church with its fairly mobile membership this get-acquainted evening proved helpful not only to my husband and me, but to the deacons and their wives as well.

Then, too, you can help the minister's wife get acquainted in the community. She may appreciate an invitation to visit a museum or some point of interest, or for a shopping tour, during her first months in her new home. Including her in some of your nonchurch activities from time to time after she's settled will provide a much-needed change of scene and will help her put down roots in the community. Oftentimes ministers' wives suffer as much from rootlessness as any other factor.

Because she will have a much wider acquaintance than the average woman, she will appreciate your leaving her "an out" when invitations are extended. On the other hand, however, do make every invitation gracious (never, "We're having the preacher and evangelist for dinner—you can come too if you wish!").

While few would want anyone to play nursemaid to them, most do appreciate kindness when husband is out of town ("May I come by for you?" or "Just call if either of us can help and we'll come running!"). In illness or on special occasions, deacons' wives may be able to see to it that neither too many pies, phone calls, or guests arrive at the parsonage, nor too few. Finding the happy medium can pose a real problem for church folk wishing to show kindness and good will, but "Where there's a woman, there's a way."

It is the law of kindness which motivates deacons and their wives to share in the entertainment of church guests. Left completely to the pastor and his wife, this can work a real hardship in time, energy, and expense. Like any hostess, if the pastor's wife does have houseguests, she will appreciate someone taking them off her hands now and then so she can catch her breath. And if, as is true in so many small churches, she is expected to house visiting evangelists, nothing would be more thoughtful than to see that her kitchen is equipped with a dishwasher. (I was staggered by a statistic on the number of dishes the average homemaker washes in her lifetime—some two million items! Add to that the extra ones the average minister's wife does, and the smaller the church the more you should add.) Some churches also budget an allowance for her use in entertaining.

Most ministers' wives feel they should do more entertaining of the congregation than they do, but often budget and energy will not permit it. Our Woman's Missionary Union council did a lovely thing recently. They wanted to sponsor a get-together primarily for the purpose of promoting fellowship among the women. I had offered our home and so they planned what they chose to call "An Evening with Martha." They took care of everything, from mailing invitations to preparing the food. I readied the house, laid the table, and made the coffee. The evening was a huge success. It was excellent people-relations for my husband and me, as well as serving the purpose of the women who planned it. In large churches a series of coffees might be just as effective.

It is kindness which keeps a Christian from looking upon the minister and his family as church property and from treating them patronizingly or as employees. Needless as this caution may seem, recently I heard of a group of suspicious deacons who felt they had to check every evening on how their new pastor was spending his time!

Kindness is also deeply appreciated when a minister is leaving, particularly if he is departing under pressure or reluctantly. His wife may have experienced fantastic pain from the time she first suspected that a move was underway to get rid of her husband. Your expressions of respect and appreciation can ease their departure somewhat.

I read of one minister pressured into retirement by a few people. Typically it was not a majority feeling, but the majority didn't have the initiative and courage to come to his defense. His son, a university student, said to a friend, "I hate the church. I despise it. Never can I forget what it did to Dad. I saw my father cry after his ouster and I vowed that no church would have any part of me!" Fortunately in this case the son later saw evidences of the people's love for his father and their desire to make amends, and he eventually entered the ministry. Oh, if only Christians could realize what they sometimes do to each other!

These laws for good pastor-people relations—acceptance, understanding, and kindness—really can be summed up under the royal law of love which applies in every Christian relationship.

And nowhere is love—an attitude of unbreakable good will— more desirable than among Christians and their spiritual leaders. The apostle John said it, and Francis Schaeffer in *The Mark of a Christian* said it again so well, "By this shall all men *(yes, including the outsiders)* know that ye are my disciples, if ye have love one for another."

Love expresses itself in patience. It shows up time and again in loyalty, especially when the pastor is under fire. It recognizes the many factors contributing to a church's shortcomings and failures, and it refuses to lay all the blame on its professional leaders.

Love insists from the outset that a pastor should—indeed must—take a day off every week. And then it encourages church members to respect his privacy on that day except in the event of genuine emergencies.

Love gives the pastor and his wife liberty to be their real selves.

Love has a listening ear and sealed lips when burdens must be shared.

Love encourages.

Love expresses appreciation, not only on anniversaries but also in the dailiness of service.

Love never freezes out another Christian when personalities clash instead of click. It is not accusing. . . .

Ideally, the pastor-people relationship should have a spiritual quality. William Douglas says: "At its best, when a minister, his wife and congregation share a common commitment and calling, the caring relationship represents a covenant. At its worst, when a minister, his wife and the congregation seek to protect individual rights and advantages against each other, there is only a contract." [5]

You and your husband are in a position to encourage a covenant relationship, to generate loving attitudes of understanding, acceptance, and kindness toward the man your church has called as its pastor.

You can help offset the lack of consideration exhibited by ill-informed and thoughtless members of your congregation.

You can help your congregation improve its understanding, and possibly revise its expectations, of the minister and his family, so that all of you can experience a togetherness in God's service which is mutually satisfying and rewarding.

6.
People Will Talk

The average woman speaks 4,800 words a day and spends one year of her life on the telephone! [1]

Possibly the biggest challenge to the wife of an active deacon is the fact that "people will talk." Because your husband is a deacon, you will have many opportunities to uphold—and sometimes defend—your church, its program, its leaders, and your fellow Christians.

How will you handle the challenge?

"Keep quiet," a deacon's wife from Tennessee suggested.

"Listen," one advised.

"But not too eagerly!" another countered.

"DO NOT GOSSIP!" one underscored large letters.

"Stay off that phone!" a pastor said emphatically.

In the biblical list of qualifications for deacons' wives, the only negative one—"not slanderers"—has to do with communicating. Paul uses a strong word here, *diabolos,* usually translated "devil." Apparently he had seen the extremely harmful effects of careless talk among believers. He warns Timothy about it in 1 Timothy 5:13, with a vivid word picture of idle women "wandering about from house to house; and not only idle, but tattlers also and busybodies, speaking things which they ought not."

Careless talk continues to do its damage. Dr. Naylor says, "Surely there is nothing that can destroy a deacon's usefulness more quickly than a wife who has a careless tongue." In strong agreement, a man who has served as pastor of medium-sized churches in Oklahoma asserted, "Careless talk on the part of deacons' wives has probably done more damage to churches than any other one thing."

Slander—making malicious statements or spreading damaging reports about another—seems utterly foreign to the Christian life. Gossip—idle talk; trifling, often groundless rumor, of a personal, sensational, or intimate nature—is unbecoming indeed to anyone!

Yet in the Scriptures we find repeated admonitions to people with problem tongues—talebearers, backbiters, whisperers, and gossips. We are warned against originating, elaborating upon, or passing on unverified reports. The reference to whispering reminds us that some things, however true, are better left unsaid. Pointing up others' weaknesses in their absence is damaging to their reputation, and digging up and relating old mistakes is usually uncalled for.

In Proverbs 6:16–19, in the list of seven things the Lord hates, three involve talk: a lying tongue; a false witness; and last, but not least, "he that soweth discord among brethren."

On the other hand, the Bible teaches that "a word fitly spoken is like apples of gold in pictures of silver." It is with words that we praise our God and confess the Lord Jesus. It is by word of mouth, primarily, that we spread the good news of the Savior.

But James compares the destruction potential of the tongue to a tiny spark of fire. If you have seen the ravages of fire caused by a mere flick of a match in a national forest, you have a vivid picture of the comparison. Those burned-over areas cannot be restored in a human lifetime! Maybe we need some "Smokey the Bear" signs around our churches to remind us of the dangers of careless talk!

The tongue is a "restless evil." In the guise of a report on an absentee or masquerading as a prayer request, comments can raise questions, make insinuations, leave false impressions. In lengthy telephone conversations the tongue tends to get loose and say things it might never mention face to face. All this in spite of our Lord's warning that at the judgment we shall each be held accountable for every idle word.

In a book titled *Did I Say That?* A. B. Simpson is quoted as saying: "I would rather play with forked lightning or take in my hands living wires, with their fiery currents, than speak a reckless word against any servant of Christ or idly repeat the slanderous darts which thousands of Christians are hurling on others." [2]

Surely it is the wise congregation which seeks out men of good report, men whose wives are discreet. For both the deacon and his wife will encounter special problems as they communicate with church members or outsiders in behalf of their church.

You will frequently find yourself the sounding board for all kinds of ideas, opinions, hearsay, and criticism, and you may be among the first to be confronted when gossip begins to fly through the membership.

Your husband will probably encounter criticism. In every congregation there seems to be someone who likes to focus on the shortcomings of the deacons! Occasionally it is a man who is not a deacon, but more often it is a woman whose husband may never be one.

I asked a number of wives how they handle such criticism. One said she did not hear much, except now and then some comment about deacons running the church. "I try to tell them this is not true. The deacons only do a lot of discussing that otherwise would have to take place in business meetings." She added wryly, "The good Lord knows there's enough done there anyway!"

It is true, sometimes deacons do become the scapegoat for churches' problems. Unfair as it is, as in all affairs of men, "it's whoever is up front who gets shot!" John J. Hurt, editor of the Texas *Baptist Standard,* advises in an editorial titled, "Withstanding Criticism": "Expect criticism. Accept it for what it is worth. Then walk among men with your chin up saying the things that need to be said, doing the things that need to be done, and trusting God."

You may be expected to reveal confidences. Sometimes, because of messages that come in over your telephone, because of actions that require your husband's absence from the home, or in the course of visits to troubled people, you will find yourself in possession of confidences which must not be violated. Assuming that you know all about church affairs, someone may pry, picking your brain for "inside information." Handling such encounters requires tact, as does any situation where you must make a refusal. Here are some suggestions from Milton Wright for saying "no" nicely:

> Make your refusal clear, definite, and final.
> Explain your reasons.
> Express your regret that you cannot comply
>   with the request.
> Accompany your refusal with some tribute to
>   the other person.[3]

When people learn that you do not make a practice of speaking for your husband or discussing others' personal affairs, they will not be likely to repeat such requests.

Some things, however, should be shared. For instance, when a major organizational change is under consideration and a woman mentions it rather negatively over coffee, you may gently share your understanding of the reasons behind the proposed change.

If a new ministry is being studied by the church and someone delivers a scorching tirade against it, you may be the only person present who can quietly justify the study. There are times when one would be traitor to her Lord and his church if she kept silence.

You certainly needn't feel compelled to speak on every subject that arises. ("Lord . . . keep me from getting talkative, and particularly from the fatal habit of thinking I must say something on every subject and on every occasion.") But you need to be well enough informed to put a stop to damaging talk and to share insights with those who are short on facts.

For in spite of all the information that goes out through your church newsletter and from the pulpit, it's amazing how poorly informed some church members are. Nothing quite equals a face-to-face discussion of issues, and deacons' wives often have the privilege and responsibility of sharing facts.

So many who come into the church are completely unaware of its program of work. I answered the phone one December morning to hear a fairly new church member ask: "Mrs. Nelson, who is this Lottie Moon? What does she need? Did she have a fire or something?" How many times our denominational vernacular must leave newcomers wondering what it's all about!

Another woman said, "Just what do you mean 'covered dish'?"

And one who'd been a church member for four years asked a friend: "What is a deacon? I see in the newsletter that your husband is one."

These questions are but a sampling of what a host of other members may have always wondered but never dared ask! Let's face it—all new members do not attend every session of their new members' classes, and all too many, both new and old, live along the outer edges of church life.

Harmony and progress depend upon an informed membership. Christians will make sacrifices for the furtherance of the kingdom if they see the sense of the sacrifice. Misinformation and misunderstanding (or no information at all) lead to discouragement, criticism, and default. We who understand the whys and wherefores must stand ready to provide and interpret information regarding the work of our church and denomination.

In snatches of conversation before and after services, in corridors—wherever people converse during the week—you can make a vital contribution by your positive support. Too frequently it is the negative note one hears in small talk about the church. Some folks seem to live in a "minor key"! Yet there are so many things happening in our churches which can be explained only in terms of God. We who are aware should be busy, as the psalmist says, "making known his deeds among the people."

This does not require undue piety on your part. A positive, wholesome perspective grows out of a sense of reverence for the things of God and a sense of gratitude "for his wonderful works to the children of men." God needs people who insist upon looking beyond the problems to the potential!

You can do immeasurable good by performing a ministry of encouragement within the church family. Christians are not exempt from the age of depression which psychiatrists say has followed close upon the heels of the age of anxiety. Discouragement steals into every fellowship—in fact, there is never a time when it isn't working on someone in the church. Sometimes it invades an entire congregation, working subtly, stealthily to undermine its power.

The ministry of encouragement calls for firm biblical understandings. About the church—the body of Christ, the kingdom visible. Its purpose—to teach and preach God's truths. Its power—the presence of the risen Christ through the Holy Spirit. Its future—"the powers of the underworld shall never overthrow it."

About our Book—God says his word shall not return unto him empty, rather it shall prosper in the purpose for which he sends it.

About the God we worship and serve—a God who cannot fail, who must prevail.

With confidence in the outcomes of faith and obedience, you **can** inspire such assurance in others. You may express it verbally **to** those who perform those thankless tasks which add to the **pleasure**, contentment, and comfort of the membership. So many **are** outside the limelight, neither expecting nor seeking recognition—the flower committee, those who work in the kitchen, the men and women who staff the nurseries, and those who work with children and youth. And there are those whose faithful presence inspires—like the little silver-haired couple who sit in that certain pew week after week. Expressing appreciation is one of the special somethings you can do. It costs nothing more than a sense of otherness, and it will bring immeasurable returns in joy.

Several years ago I discovered Thank-U-Grams, a telegram-style stationery distributed by The Kimball Foundation.* "There's magic in a word of praise," these little missives remind both sender and recipient. It's remarkable how much appreciation can be expressed in a matter of seconds and in less than fifty words!   (*24 Northcate Drive, Brentwood, Missouri 73144.)

Of course, encouragement does not always require verbal expression. The way you participate in a worship service can encourage or discourage. Georgia Harkness deplores a 'deadpan' apathy on the part of a congregation and suggests that "polite passivity" may be one of the most impregnable barriers to the Holy Spirit's working in a church.[4]

The way you respond to a conference leader's leadership, the way you cooperate, can be heartening. A look, a smile, a leaning-forward as you listen, a pat on the hand can encourage. Merely sitting beside some lonely or troubled one and after service wishing her a good week ahead can give renewed courage.

There is encouragement, too, in forgiveness. When we are disappointed in fellow Christians who have been delinquent in their duties, we must be willing to forgive. To be made to feel wanted and needed, to be given a second chance after one has erred—this is to be encouraged. People need to feel our acceptance, and they need repeated opportunities to contribute of themselves. The Bible teaches that we have no right to say of any member of the body of Christ, "We have no need of thee." You and your husband may be able to express encouragement through your hospitality or through enlisting the delinquent's assistance in some church-related task. So often, I fear, Christians are delinquent because they are like square pegs in round holes in the positions nominating committees have requested them to fill. Churches need intelligent personnel counseling as desperately as businesses if they are to cut down on absenteeism and worker-turnover.

The ministry of encouragement is scriptural. Remember how in Isaiah 4:6–7 "They helped every one his neighbour; and every one said to his brother, Be of good courage. So the carpenter encouraged the goldsmith, and he that smootheth with the hammer him that smote the anvil."

"But who's going to encourage me?" you may be asking. "Sometimes I get terribly discouraged myself!"

David, a man after God's own heart, had the problem, too. But look at his solution in 1 Samuel 30:6: "And David was greatly distressed; for the people spake of stoning him, because the soul of all the people was grieved, every man for his sons and for his daughters: but *David encouraged himself in the Lord his God.*"

It was this same man who said in Psalm 27:13–14: "I had fainted (lost heart) unless I had believed to see the goodness of the Lord in the land of the living. *Wait on the Lord: be of good courage, and he shall strengthen thine heart.*"

Another ministry which you can perform above and beyond your routine responsibilities is the ministry of listening. I imagine it was the women of the Jerusalem church who called the apostles' attention to the fact that the Grecian widows were being neglected. And I would venture to guess that most of the needs with which pastors and deacons are confronted today come to their attention through women.

"Little Mrs. Beech has been hospitalized; young Joe Brown is experimenting with drugs. The Smiths have had a death in the family, and the Joneses need financial assistance." It is usually a woman who is first to hear and to pass on the information to the church office, her husband, or the pastor.

You may be of specific help to your husband and pastor as you listen to what women are saying to each other. A denominational worker, formerly a pastor, says deacons' wives are in a better position than anyone else to discover dissatisfaction that is brewing. He noted that women are apt to express themselves more freely than men, who tend to keep still while hostility breeds within them. The wise deacon's wife can discern whether what she hears will likely die a natural death ("where no wood is, the fire goeth out"), or whether it sounds like a "storm warning." She can quietly discuss it with her husband who in turn may talk it over with the pastor in time for a crisis to be averted. Gaines S. Dobbins notes how leaders in the Jerusalem church moved to avert a crisis: they recognized the "murmuring"; all the facts of the case were obtained; an unbiased committee known as "the seven" were appointed; and the problem was solved before it disrupted the fellowship.[5]

By way of the grapevine you may learn of needs that should receive the attention of church leaders. Many a pastor has been grateful to hear from a good deacon's wife that certain individuals need a visit or that certain talk should be squelched immediately. This is a constructive use of gossip.

A woman, listening with her heart, gains insight into people's lives. As she greets people with sincere interest, she may come upon troubled persons sorely in need of ministry. She may discover some who are frustrated misfits in their elected positions

and she may call this to the attention of appropriate leaders. Or
listening, she may have the joy of discovering talents—gifts just
waiting for a chance at expression.

Because deacons and their wives are usually community-ori-
ented, they can do much to help build a good reputation for their
church. A part of any church's reputation depends upon what
its members say about it. Outsiders are curious, and they listen
to discover what our church is like and what it means to us.

Recently a woman from another faith said to me: "I sat beside
a young woman from one of your churches at a banquet last
Monday. She said her church had 1,300 in Sunday School the day
before!" She was obviously impressed and was relaying to others
some excellent publicity for that church!

Your church's statistical record may not be so impressive, but
it may foster a splendid day-care program. Several members help
with the community's "Meals on Wheels." A group visits a
rehabilitation center regularly. Johnny and his Sunday School
class took a field trip to a synagogue. Your church bus makes the
rounds in a newcomer's neighborhood. Your facilities are being
used certain weekdays by the county health department. Six new
deacons were ordained last Sunday. . . .

Don't keep this news as inside information! Tell it around.
Include your church in your small talk! This is the best kind of
public relations program a church can have.

Out in the business world I found small talk about my church
was well-received. Often it encouraged other Christians to talk
of theirs. Frequently it gave me a chance to clear up some common misconceptions about my denomination. Sometimes it provided an opening for a direct, positive witness for Christ.

Needless to say, certain information should be kept inside the
church family. Yet all Christians do not realize this—in factory
towns it is not unusual for everything that goes on in the church
business meeting to be common knowledge by everyone on the

assembly line half an hour after they get to work the next morning. As we often told our children, "Some things we discuss are for family consumption only!"

Yes, people—including you—will talk. As a deacon's wife, you are in a privileged position to communicate in your church's behalf. When your relationship with the Lord and his people is warm and vital, it should not be a fearful responsibility. For with your heart you'll listen, and out of a heart diligently kept you will speak.

Love as a fruit of the Spirit, says Harry A. DeWire in *The Christian as Communicator*, makes a difference "in the way we speak . . . in the things we hear . . . in the way our eyes fall upon another . . . in our greeting. . . . It affects the total make-up of the body. . . ." [6]

As you grow in love, the Christ in you will come through gently in your conversation. You'll be like the good wife in Proverbs who "openeth her mouth with wisdom and in her tongue is the law of kindness."

Meanwhile, as you mature, pray with the psalmist as in Psalm 141:3: "Set a watch, O Lord, before my mouth; keep the door of my lips" And as in Psalm 19:14: "Let the words of my mouth, and the meditations of my heart, be acceptable in thy sight, O Lord, my strength, and my redeemer."

7.
Your Supporting Role

"Support is another word for love and love is woman's métier."

Ashley Montagu

Your helping, supportive relationship to your deacon-husband can be whatever you and he wish to make it. Of course, if you are already deeply involved in a leadership role in the church, or if your home or work responsibilities at the moment are particularly heavy, you may not be able to take on additional activities. Support, however, does not necessarily require action.

But if you have never quite found your special place of usefulness in the body of Christ, it may be that teaming up with your husband in his ministries will be the most satisfying and productive way you can give time and energy in the Lord's service.

Traditionally, deacons and their wives have assisted with the church ordinances. Helpers behind the scenes of the ceremonies of baptism and the Lord's Supper are indispensable. We shall never forget the deacon who came to the rescue with his fist and a diaper hastily confiscated from the nursery when the baptistry sprang a leak just before a service! Nor the deacon's wife who pitched in with bucket and mop after her husband decided to help the custodian by turning on the water to fill the baptistry —and then forgot to turn it off! It was a deacon behind the scenes who stopped one candidate from entering the baptistry clad only in his shorts, and it was a deacon's wife who comforted a shivering little girl until someone retrieved her dry undies from her mother's purse in the church auditorium.

But seriously, the new believer needs a genuinely caring person to assist in preparation for this once-in-a-lifetime experience. No matter how thoroughly the pastor has instructed them, many candidates still need reassurance.

Unless it is an otherwise designated responsibility, the deacons and their wives will want to see to it that the dressing rooms are clean, well lighted, and well ventilated. They can see that the arrangements provide for privacy, that hair dryers are available, and that the robes and supplies are clean and ready for use.

One deacon's wife told me: "Of all the work I've done about the church, I believe my greatest blessing comes as I help new Christians prepare for baptism. To have a part in this sacred experience—to see the shining, happy faces afterward—brings the kind of joy a pastor must feel as he baptizes them."

In the observance of the Lord's Supper in most churches the deacons and their wives assume responsibility for its preparation. The elements must be secured, cups and trays polished, linens laundered. Deacons' wives say they feel a special sense of reverence as they perform these simple acts. What a contrast to the woman in a conclave of women's liberationists who hooted, "And to think the church relegates these menial tasks to modern women who never lay a hand to their own linens!"

I'll never forget the way one deacon's wife ironed the fine linen cloth for the Lord's Supper table in a church in the Missouri Ozarks. It glimmered from the touch of her iron in the filtered light of those special Sunday mornings, its folds making an abstract in white when it was laid open. That same deacon's wife baked the unleavened bread for the service, carefully scoring it into perfect squares. In whatever she did for her church, only her best was good enough. One could sense all that she did was done lovingly and obediently, as the Lord taught, "in remembrance of me."

We have come a long way from the example of our Lord who stooped to wash the disciples' feet when we begin to feel we're too good, too high and mighty, to perform the humble acts necessary for observing the church ordinances. We have come a long way from his teachings about service if we find ourselves wondering, when some form of service is requested, "Can't we pay someone to do that?"

Through the centuries, from tabernacle to Temple to our present-day churches, Edith Deen pictures "devout women serving God's holy meeting place where and when needed, no matter how menial the task. For centuries their fidelity and zeal have inspired church-goers, helping them to remember that in the midst of indifference and infidelity to God, there always are those who render homage to him in small, seemingly insignificant ways." [1] Certainly this is a tradition we will want to keep alive until the day our Lord returns.

When you find out how the deacons in your church are organized, and on which committee your husband is serving, you will see where you can be of assistance. In many churches deacons are organized with a leader for the following tasks: proclamation, community relations, family care, and fellowship.[2]

It is suggested that the proclamation leader seek opportunities for deacons to witness and preach; that he promote deacon involvement in revival meetings and other evangelistic efforts of the church. You can easily see that the wife of a man working in this area would feel some special responsibility for accompanying him in his own witnessing and speaking efforts when feasible. She would want to train for witnessing, and many churches have excellent training now available for lay evangelism. (In fact, I believe every deacon's wife would benefit from this training as it will help her in every life relationship to give a witness for her Lord.) She could help too in personally promoting her church's evangelism program in the course of her own activities and among her neighbors and acquaintances.

The fellowship leader is concerned with improving church fellowship. He will make plans for fellowship among deacons and their wives, too. A wife's point of view can be most helpful as she and her husband put their heads together to discuss ways the fellowship can be improved. In most cases she and other wives will be needed to help implement the plans. Once in a while, the men will do it themselves, but that's the exception rather than the rule!

A third leader is charged with strengthening community and church relations. The woman active in school affairs and in various other community organizations can be of special assistance here. If she participates in the missions organization of her church (and hopefully every deacon's wife is concerned about, if not deeply involved in, missionary education and action), she will often be able to suggest ways the church can initiate or tie into community efforts in behalf of people of special need and circumstance. Sometimes, in a husband-wife brainstorming session an embryo of an idea thrown out may spark ideas from which a great ministry is born.

The fourth area in which your husband may serve is family care. In many churches every deacon assumes responsibility for a particular group of families, so let's look at this one a little more closely.

Take Steve Meyers, for example. He and the other deacons in his church have each accepted responsibility for a specific group of church families. They want every family to know their church is interested in them, and they feel their visits, representing the church, will build the fellowship, tie on members, and reduce the number who become inactive or apathetic. They have set themselves a goal of at least three visits to every family per year.

Sarah, his wife, is really sold on their plans. Long before her husband was elected, she had been concerned about the need for strengthening the church family through personal attention to its members. She knew her pastor could not possibly look after every single family. This group plan seemed to be a place to take hold and begin to do something specific.

Before his first round of visits, Steve asked Sarah if she'd go along with him. Of course, it would take time and a little effort, but she couldn't help thinking that their going together on these visits might give them companionship in a cause bigger than themselves. It seemed so many of their activities separated rather than drew them together. So she'd arranged for a sitter for the children, planned her day around their "date," and served a simple dinner that evening.

They were pleasantly surprised at the warm welcome they received on these get-acquainted visits. On the way home, as they relaxed over coffee at the pancake house, they made plans for further contacts with the families in their group.

Steve suggested a backyard cookout, and Sarah mentioned the possibility of all the families in the group eating out together after church some Sunday. She thought, too, she might plan a morning coffee for the ladies.

"I didn't know the Skaggs family had a retarded son," Steve remarked.

"And Linda Brown's a nurse at City Hospital—now I see why she can't be at church every single Sunday!" Sarah exclaimed.

"That little Mrs. Meeks, there's not a more faithful member when it comes to Sunday morning worship—but no one really knows her. Maybe now she'll have someone to turn to when trouble comes. You know, it's these people who never join a Sunday School class or a missions group who will benefit most from a deacon's interest." Steve was catching a vision of the real need for this kind of family ministry.

"Sarah," Steve asked, "couldn't you give me a hand with the records on our group? You know how my work is—all day and

half some nights, too. And you know how impatient I get with
details. If you could help me keep up with these families, it'd be
a tremendous help . . . it's something you could do evenings
when I must work."

The record forms were simple enough—one with a place for
family names, birthdays, when they joined the church, and so on.
There was a monthly report form for listing visits and other
contacts. And a monthly calendar sheet with two or three lines
for each day where birthdays, anniversaries, weddings, and so
forth could be listed. Actually, Sarah thought, I could get greeting cards in quantity and in one sitting each month address them
and mark them for mailing on certain dates.

"We must remember the Jones wedding," Sarah said. "Do you
think we could plan to attend?"

"Someone from church should be there," Steve said. "Being
in a church across town, most won't go."

"I keep thinking about that retarded child," Sarah said.
"Surely there's some help available for that family. . . ."

And Steve made a mental note to discuss referral possibilities
with the pastor.

There are other ways you can help in the family care ministry.
You can be on the lookout in the newspapers for special honors
members of your group may receive. If it's a business honor, you
can clip the item and send it along with congratulations from
your husband. Clippings about community achievements might
be posted on the church bulletin board. If the church newsletter
has room for commendations on achievements of members, you
might call the church office with the information.

Sometimes your husband may come across widows and divor-
cees in need of special counseling, and now and then a man out
of work, and often he will be in position to refer them. He may
be able to help a teen-ager find part-time work, and families are
most appreciative of interest in their youngsters. You may be

familiar with books which would be of help, and you may secure paperbacks for giving, or else borrow books from the church or public library for loaning.

As you see, many little tasks can well be carried on by "wife Friday" if she has a mind to help. Certainly if her husband is heavily involved in his work and in church and community affairs, he will need her help as surely as he needs the help of his assistants at work. Many of these little, seemingly insignificant tasks are ways of saying, "You are important to us, and your church really does care about you." There's no way for a church to care, you know, except through its people.

One busy physician says his wife is very helpful in reminding him of his responsibilities—calling his office, for instance, to remind him of meetings. A businessman appreciates his wife representing him when he is out of town—"she makes a point of being at business and prayer meetings when I can't be there. She keeps in touch with my families and attends special occasions like weddings and funerals even if I can't go along. She's also good about visiting group members who may be hospitalized in my absence."

A Fort Worth deacon paid a high tribute to his wife, saying: "When I serve on a church committee, my wife does, too, really putting more of herself and time into it than I am willing or able to."

Not until the final records are opened will we know the extent of laymen's contributions to the establishment of new churches. Pastors have repeatedly turned to their faithful, reliable deacons to go forth from their churches to provide aggressive leadership in preaching points and missions. When this kind of opportunity arises, the strength of the family partnership is really tested. Usually it must be a "*we'll* go" response, with wife as well as deacon willing to sacrifice deep and meaningful ties with the mother church.

Many military deacons and their wives have pitched in to open and strengthen work in pioneer areas. These people don't wait to put down roots; they just dig in and get the job done. Behind many successes in denominational outreach are husband-wife teams, many of whom have become involved through the special concern of a sensitive feminine partner.

A Mississippian who has led out in lay involvement in his denomination, and one of the host of laymen who have made significant financial contributions to work in pioneer areas, says, "My wife has done much to encourage me to greater mission involvement."

I have been impressed with the support of some wives who cannot serve alongside their husbands in their ministries for the Lord. One, with a severe case of arthritis, was known throughout her church for her prayer support. Another, a home-bound invalid, was extremely generous in permitting her husband to spend many Sunday afternoons helping develop Sunday Schools in his area.

It is a fortunate church whose deacons with jack-of-all-trades skills have wives who encourage them to help with whatever needs doing. A woman from Texas tells how one sweltering Saturday two sweating, grease-covered deacons worked to repair the leak in the copper cooling coil of the church air conditioner, making it possible for their church to worship and study in comfort the next day and saving the congregation the expense of a new $2,500 unit.

Countless times we have gone by the church during off hours to find a dedicated deacon working at something which we didn't even realize needed attention. I know that often behind such scenes are wives who may have had to change their plans for the day or evening. For frequently family matters must wait when a deacon spends his leisure hours serving his church.

If your husband takes his role seriously, you will find he will often need and welcome your moral support. When the church is pastorless, he may assume duties ordinarily cared for by the pastor. If he is chairman, he carries a heavy burden for the ongoing of the church. Hopefully, this honor and place of responsibility will be reserved until he is a mature Christian and has had wide experience in many phases of the church's work. It is a heavier task than the non-deacon realizes.

Your support may be most helpful when he is discouraged or disappointed. With that feminine intuitive insight that's unusually keen when combined with love, you will know when he needs to express his hurts or resentments, when he needs to be comforted or challenged, when he needs a bit of mothering or a lover, when he needs silence, a sounding board, or a sparring partner. Dr. Naylor says: "He is going to come home from many church meetings when he needs the prayerful encouragement of somebody who loves him. It is no time to sit down and have a good critical talk fest about the shortcomings of the membership. It is time to talk about the blessings of the Lord and the privileges of serving God and how well God has wrought and how greatly he has blessed. A time to remember the trials through which he has safely led. These are the hours when the need is to talk about good things."

If you happen to be a more mature Christian than he, don't ever pull your rank on him. Don't ever, ever indicate you think you're the superior Christian. But if your father was a pastor or a deacon, you may be able to provide insights and give the intangible support he needs in difficult times.

None of us can be all things to all people. There is a definite limit to the number of people whom we can genuinely help at any given time. But each of us can do something. You may want to take an inventory right now, evaluating what you can contribute to this partnership-extraordinaire.

You may want to use the evaluation suggested by Peter

Drucker for persons in a business-team relationship. Ask your-self:

> What is the most important contribution that
>   I can make to the perfection of our team?
> What self-development do I need?
> What knowledge and skill do I have to acquire
>   to make the contribution I should be making?
> What strengths do I have to put to work?
> What standards do I have to set for myself? [3]

And you will want to add, "What would the Master have me do?"

"To focus on contribution," says Mr. Drucker, "is to focus on effectiveness." Your contribution to your special team will be uniquely yours. It will depend largely on the role your husband assumes as a deacon, upon his special interests, his spiritual gifts. Your interest and gifts will enhance his.

Together you have something to offer that no other partner-ship ever could.

8.
That Caring Touch

It is time for women to take the church into their arms so Christians may know once more the true meaning of "church family."

Can you imagine a home where only the barest essentials to life receive attention?

Food, yes—but always the plainest, with never a touch of beauty or a hint of spice. Furnishings, of course—chairs, tables, beds, but no pictures to please the eye, no plants to ease the bareness, no curtains to gentle the midday light.

Care for the children, certainly. Baths, but no fun along with them. No listening ear, no affectionate hugs, no encouraging looks, no tenderness or comfort.

No welcomes or good-bys. No thank you's or please's. No gifts. No celebrations. Only the absolute essentials!

Women are family- and home-makers, specially suited to providing those caring touches to a house and the people who live in it. Maria Waser said it so beautifully, "Feminine hands have, from time immemorial, lighted Christmas trees, filled gardens with flowers, and even transformed cemeteries into joyful gardens." [1]

Women not only provide caring touches to their environment, but they bring out the "caring" in their men! Someone has said that, but for women, men would live only in monasteries or barracks or slums. Men, roughing the wilds of a frontier put up with the barest bed-and-board arrangements until they send for their wives. Then, suddenly seeing their surroundings through the eyes of a woman, they begin to fix things up. And women, coming on the scene, tend to "gentle" their men.

Jesus on many occasions commended women for their caring touch. He praised the woman who washed his feet with her tears, expressing her devotion in a courtesy neglected by his host. He defended the Mary who lavished a costly ointment upon him when men standing by objected to such waste. Withdrawing from his male companions, he responded frequently to the loving hospitality of Mary and Martha. He respected the very feminine qualities of these women who saw to the gracious extras which make life serene and joyful, and he idealized them for women down through the centuries.

The church family and its home—its meeting place—need a woman's caring touch. By virtue of her husband's leadership position, the respected deacon's wife can often give informal leadership in the family and homemaking tasks that transform the people of a church into a loving family, their meeting house into a beloved home.

The qualities which women may bring to this need are not necessarily feminine. A husband may be more gentle, affectionate, and perceptive, with a deeper sense of the aesthetic, than his wife. But these are qualities for which women have traditionally been known, possibly because women have had more time to devote to these things than men, busy with their bread-and-butter responsibilities.

Women with their creativity can bring beauty to their churches. Years ago I clipped an article titled, "A Church Should Look Loved," in which Rose Burket says, "Churches, like people, must have love or they wither." Visitors to a church, she says, can sense whether or not it is loved by its people. In her travels she saw churches with dull brass and dingy walls. She observed choir members with their robes carelessly thrown on, **detracting** from carefully prepared music. She visited one church with rich red carpeting, spotlessly clean, but there at the front of the auditorium stood the vacuum cleaner patiently awaiting the next cleaning day! [2]

Most church auditoriums are carefully kept. But some educational areas! A church, I believe, should reflect at least as high a housekeeping standard as the average home in the community. Its lawn and planters should be at least as carefully kept as those of most of its members.

In fact, the house of God and its grounds should receive better care than any other house in town! You, as a deacon's wife, may want to look at your church with an awakened eye. Sometimes one woman who really cares can gently nudge the right person to get the job done. In some cases she may enlist other women to help her improve the appearance of the place your congregation calls "home." Or, beginning in an area for which you are responsible as an elected worker, you can set an example others will follow.

While flowers are not essential to worship, they are a way of honoring the Lord's presence among us. Deacons' wives sometimes serve on the flower committee. In churches whose budgets will not cover a weekly order to a florist, creative women find ingenious ways to add that caring touch, to express appreciation to God for making such lavish gifts of beauty to mankind. Rose Burket found a loaf of homemade bread and four shiny red apples composing an appealing worship center in a rural church. Many women care enough to think ahead and plant glads and mums and zinnias for use in their churches. Women who care study flower arranging for churches so they'll be assured of following principles of good taste in dignifying the service with their arrangements.

Deacons' wives with a gift for meal planning, preparation, and service can provide that caring touch to the fellowship meals of their churches. Nowhere is woman's caring touch more evident, or more sorely missed, than in the serving of meals. "We smile, sometimes, at the church supper," Elton Trueblood writes, "but we are not wise when we do so. It is the oldest Christian ritual. It is one spontaneous way of expressing the reality of *koinonia.*" He goes so far as to say that it may be even more valuable than Sunday worship. "If we were truly wise we should build on this sound base rather than despise it, for the church supper can become a love feast." [3]

The fellowship dinners each Wednesday, prepared by some of the young women of our church, have taken on the spirit of a love feast. These women know our people pay dearly for atmosphere when they eat out, and they have found it neither extremely expensive nor terribly time-consuming to create atmosphere at our church meals. The food they cook would be just as nutritious served in paper plates on butcher paper, but they use dinnerware, and for informal meals each table is spread with bright checked flannel-back table covers and centered with candles in decorative bottles or a variety of seasonal decorations. On more festive occasions the dining room is softened with pink plisse cloths and appropriate centerpieces. Contributing to ease in conversation, the tables are set up singly rather than in stiff banquet style, and the menus are full of surprises, often with a special treat for the children seated at their small tables.

Add to all this the smell of good things cooking, a pleasant greeting from the deacon and his wife who handle the finances, and a view of the girls in the kitchen looking as though they have had the time of their life getting dinner for a crowd, top it off with singing and prayer around the tables afterward, and you've got fellowship!

Even as I write these lines, two women of our church (they happen to be deacons' wives) are planning and promoting a Thanksgiving dinner to be held in our church dining room following the Sunday morning worship service. They will spend hours on the phone, in shopping and food preparation before the week is out. Before they're finished, the dining room will be transformed with colorful symbols of the harvest. A great many church families who never have much opportunity to visit will enjoy a couple of hours together that day, and the fellowship of the church will be strengthened.

Just as something is missing in a home which does not celebrate, so the church misses something without celebrations. "Celebration has a happy sound. The sound of fellowship rings out when *celebration* is spoken. *Celebration* rings of rejoicing people, notable occasions, festivities, and continuity of a worthy past." [4]

Women are celebration-makers, and there needn't be an important occasion for celebration to occur—the midweek supper can be a celebration. Anniversaries, farewells, the honoring of retiring staff members, the coming of new members; all of these call for celebration. Celebrations meet a real human need, they make tradition and memories. Memories and tradition make families of people, and homes out of houses.

Like many other churches, three times a year we go all out with a missions celebration. Many come to the missions dinners costumed to the occasion. "Fall Roundup," as we call our Colorado missions emphasis, is one of the most joyous occasions of the year as young and old appear in Western wear for chuckwagon fare and singing 'round the campfire. At these celebrations missions information is presented attractively and appealingly to many who are not personally involved in the missions organizations.

Children love celebrations, too, and one gaining in popularity is the children's "Birthday Party for Jesus" at Christmas time. Last year a hundred children attended the first of these in our church, bringing brand-new games and toys in holiday wrappings marked according to age-level for distribution to less-fortunate boys and girls. It was a birthday party in the truest sense, with small group games directed by teen-agers, cake, candles, ice cream, tables gaily decorated, and for the climax, a film telling the old, old story of the birth of our Savior. This year children from a mission across town and those in nearby apartments will also be invited to share in this child-style celebration.

Celebrations help members to form deep, meaningful, and durable relationships with one another and the church. While they are no more a distinctive responsibility for deacons' wives than any other activity, you as a key woman in your church can help in the making of such memorable occasions. Never underestimate your influence as a Christian woman!

But, as the writer of Proverbs 17:1 declares, "Better a dry crust and concord with it than a house full of feasting and strife" (NEB). Better no fellowship meals at all, if within the church kitchen gossip, criticism, and pessimism go into the preparation! Better no celebrations whatsoever, if the celebration of worship is neglected! Better a dirty church house than self-centered worshipers stained with sin and foul attitudes!

Jesus reminds us, in Luke 10:41-42, that we Marthas can become too absorbed in the more tangible aspects of our home-making tasks. "Martha, Martha," he said, "you are fretting and fussing about so many things; but one thing is necessary." He looked down at Mary, seated at his feet, listening to him, and said, ". . . but one thing is necessary. The part that Mary has chosen is best; and it shall not be taken away from her" (NEB).

In *People Who Care*, C. W. Brister points out that Christian concern (caring) is not merely an activity. "It is a fundamental attitude or disposition motivated by the love of God and needs of persons. It is a matter of *being*, of risking oneself even in alien relationships, then of *doing* something constructive for one's neighbor.[5]

You as a deacon's wife can provide informal leadership in

helping the women of the church major on its most vital caring tasks. For one thing, you can help create an atmosphere of warmth and welcome. Georgia Harkness says this atmosphere of friendly fellowship is one "the layman—*and perhaps more readily the lay woman*—can create or destroy." [6]

Corporate worship—and indeed every aspect of church life—is enriched by friendliness. Visitors and new members honor us by their presence, and we honor them by making them welcome. True, in suburban and metropolitan churches one does not always know who's a member and who's a guest. But this should not preclude a greeting. Sometimes we do well, I think, to admit our ignorance and begin to get acquainted with the stranger sitting nearby.

Welcome involves more than the briefest greeting. Introductions of other members are in order. Visitors sometimes like to be shown around the church buildings. And a follow-up visit in the home is unequaled in extending a true welcome on behalf of the church. If in every church, large and small, deacons' wives assumed a personal responsibility for welcome, no one need ever say, "What an unfriendly church!"

Women have a reputation for simplicity, unguardedness, and naturalness which makes them a "natural" for building fellowship in a church. It is this spontaneity which causes a woman to take her pastor's hand in both of hers and say what she has really felt as he preached . . . that prompts her to embrace a little old lady starving for a human touch . . . that draws her to the timid little boy . . . that causes her to smile across the room to a young woman looking so lonely and ill at ease.

It is woman's spontaneity which causes her to say of some worthy effort under consideration, "Let's do it!" while man's prudence suggests caution. Dr. Trueblood says, "One of the most harmful forces in the spiritual life may be the counsel of prudence." Prudence, he says, can damage the spirit of adventure so sorely needed in some of our churches these days.[7]

The sensitivity of the deacon's wife is also invaluable to her church. As you get to know other members better, at times you may sense inner needs and either help alleviate their problem or put them in touch with someone who can.

Your sensitivity makes you gentle. As one deacon mentioned, women are "naturals" with children and youth, and you may be needed in this area. Little children and awkward teen-agers from broken or loveless homes so desperately need someone to really care. And they need someone to care about! In your visits with your husband, you may be able to provide that caring touch for the children of the home while he and the parents are busy discussing adult matters. You may encourage the father and mother determined not to attend Sunday School to permit the children to do so. In many cases the woman of the troubled family to whom your husband may be ministering may need nothing so desperately as another woman's friendship.

Your sensitivity can help create a climate of concern within the church, not only for children but for rebellious teen-agers and for the growing numbers of aging in our communities. Often the ministries of men come about as a result of woman's sensitivity. You may be keenly aware of a community need which will require innovative ministry on the part of your church. It may be a need women alone cannot handle, but with the endorsement of a group of men like the deacons the church may be led to launch out in faith. Just as a good mother leads her family in concern for others, so a deacon's wife may stimulate her church to be like the good wife in Proverbs who "reacheth out her hands to the poor, yea, she stretcheth forth her hands to the needy."

It has been said that to know is to care, to care is to pray, and to pray is to give. Women, with a tradition of interest in missions, have spent many hours in the study of Christian missions, work for which most men have little time. Because women have come to know about world needs and Jesus' teaching concerning our responsibility, they have come to care. Only eternity will reveal the measure of their influence in men's providing the necessary resources to meet world needs. In your concern for missions, you can directly and indirectly provide that caring touch for a hurting world.

The deacon's wife can bring her prayers to the needs of the church. If women sin differently from men, they also pray differently. Your caring prayer in behalf of your husband on a difficult assignment may literally move mountains. As you and your husband pray together, you may mention spiritual needs of the church which otherwise might not come to his attention.

It is the woman in the home who is primarily responsible for nurture, and the deacon's wife can bring her abilities along this line to the nurturing of weaker members of the church, especially women. Going out of your way to include a timid young woman in activities of the women's organization, taking time to explain denominational jargon to the new convert, going by for the newcomer hesitant about showing up for a meeting in the house of a stranger, being gracious and helpful to wives of new deacons —all of these nurturing activities can best be carried on by women.

Like a family, a congregation should take pride in its heritage as a local body and as a denomination. And just as the woman in a good home cherishes her family and nurtures within them a family pride, so your example of stedfast devotion and staunch loyalty will lead others to cherish their church. In contrast to many men conditioned by experiences out in the cold, harsh business world, women seem to have an implicit faith in the ultimate outcome of God's workings and can spread serenity and hope when things seem to be going from bad to worse.

Your lively, consistent, contagious faith, in fact, will be the greatest contribution you can make to your deacon-husband and your church. This, with the supreme virtue of love, can bring immeasurable blessing to all it touches. The church, the bride of Christ, needs to love the Lord with the kind of love women know how to give, love that makes a total commitment, that is self-abandoning, optimistic, and completely loyal.

No two deacons' wives are alike in what they have to offer their church. But each of you has potential which God can develop and use in cooperation with your deacon-husband.

You and your husband have a blessing many couples cannot claim. You have a common denominator in your love for Jesus Christ and his church. What a blessing to be able to share this love with one another!

What a challenge now that he has been set aside as a special servant of the church to minister and to promote harmony! What an opportunity for togetherness, for *team!*

They tell me it's a myth that "behind every good man is a good woman." But I dare anyone to try to prove that the married deacon is not a better one with the love and support of a good wife!

Growth and fulfilment await the man who accepts in all seriousness the responsibilities which accompany ordination. And, to the extent she wishes, rewards await the wife by his side.

NOTES

Scripture quotations marked NEB are from *The New English Bible*, New Testament, Second Edition. © The Delegates of the Oxford University Press, and the Syndics of the Cambridge University Press 1961, 1970. Reprinted by permission.

Scripture quotations marked *The Living Bible* are from *The Living Bible, Paraphrased* (Wheaton: Tyndale House Publishers, 1971) and are used by permission.

Chapter 1
[1] Elton Trueblood, "Equipping the Layman for Increasing Responsibility," *Home Missions,* November, 1969, p. 18.
[2] Owen Cooper, "My Fellow Deacons," *Rocky Mountain Baptist,* July 28, 1972, p. 4.
[3] Howard B. Foshee, *The Ministry of the Deacon* (Nashville: Convention Press, 1968), p. 4.
[4] Robert E. Naylor, *The Baptist Deacon* (Nashville: Broadman Press, 1955), p. 11. (Other quotations from Naylor are also from *The Baptist Deacon.*)
[5] C. W. Brister, *People Who Care* (Nashville: Broadman Press, 1967), p. 18.

Chapter 2
[1] Kenneth Chafin, *Help I'm a Layman* (Waco: Word, 1966), p. 23.
[2] Adela Rogers St. Johns, "Women's Lib—and other nonsense," *The Denver Post,* January 23, 1972, p. 7.
[3] Watchman Nee, *Sit Walk Stand* (London: Victory Press, 1957), p. 12.
[4] Elizabeth O'Connor, *Eighth Day of Creation—Gifts and Creativity* (Waco: Word Books), p. 40.
[5] John Hendrix, "Discovering Your Gifts and Calling Forth the Gifts of Others," *The Deacon,* April–June, 1972, p. 24.

Chapter 3
[1] Paul Plattner, *Conflict and Understanding in Marriage* (Richmond: John Knox Press, 1950), p. 29.
[2] Alice Patricia Hershey, "Put Him in His Place, Wife," *The Marriage Affair,* ed. J. Allan Petersen (Wheaton: Tyndale House, 1971), p. 92.
[3] Foshee, *op. cit.,* p. 32.
[4] Georgia Harkness, *The Church and Its Laity* (Nashville: Abingdon, 1962), p. 94.
[5] Mollie Hart, *When Your Husband Retires* (New York: Appleton-Century-Crofts, 1960), pp. 123–4.
[6] Bobby S. Terry, "How Deacons Are Training in the Bluegrass State," *The Deacon,* January–March, 1971, pp. 8–9.

[7] David H. Smith, "How Deacons Lead," *The Deacon*, October–December, 1970, pp. 48–49.

Chapter 4
[1] Evelyn Mills Duvall, *Family Development* (Philadelphia: J. B. Lippincott, 1962), p. 430.
[2] Edith Deen, *The Bible's Legacy for Womanhood* (Garden City: Doubleday, 1969).
[3] General Mills, Inc., *Betty Crocker's Hostess Cookbook* (New York: Golden Press, 1967).
[4] Elizabeth Swadley, *Dinner on the Ground Cookbook* (Nashville: Broadman Press, 1972), preface and p. 127.

Chapter 5
[1] Elizabeth Dodds, "What Are You Doing to Your Minister's Wife?" *Good Housekeeping*, June, 1959, p. 89.
[2] Bryant M. Kirkland, "The Art of Ministerial Succession," *Pastoral Psychology*, December, 1968, p. 20.
[3] Wallace Denton, *Ministers' Wives* (New York: Harper & Row, 1965).
    William Douglas, *The Role of the Minister's Wife* (Philadelphia: Westminster, 1962).
[4] Dorothy Harrison Pentecost, *The Pastor's Wife and the Church* (Chicago: Moody Press, 1964), p. 40.
[5] Douglas, *op. cit.*, p. 184.

Chapter 6
[1] The President's Message, *The Pen Woman*, October, 1972.
[2] Leslie B. Flynn, *Did I Say That?* (Nashville: Broadman Press, 1959), p. 34.
[3] Milton Wright, *The Art of Conversation* (New York: Whittlesey House, 1936), pp. 287–88.
[4] Harkness, *op. cit.*, p. 95.
[5] Gaines S. Dobbins, "The Deacon and Church Harmony," *The Deacon*, April–June, 1971, p. 20.
[6] Harry DeWire, *The Christian as Communicator* (Philadelphia: Westminster Press, 1961), p. 124.

Chapter 7
[1] Deen, *op. cit.*, p. 64.
[2] "The Deacon Family Ministry Plan," a pamphlet published by The Sunday School Board of the Southern Baptist Convention (Nashville, 1972).
[3] Peter Drucker, *The Effective Executive* (New York: Harper and Row, 1966), p. 70.

Chapter 8

[1] Plattner, *op. cit.*, p. 90

[2] Rose Burket, "A Church Should Look Loved," *Church Administration*, November 1962, p. 14.

[3] Trueblood, *op. cit.*, pp. 71–72.

[4] Howard B. Foshee, editorial, *Church Administration*, August, 1972, p. 3.

[5] Brister, *op. cit.*, p. 47.

[6] Harkness, *loc. cit.*

[7] Trueblood, *op. cit.*, p. 106.